Fashion Foundations

CRE

& DESIGN

Dress, Body, Culture

Series Editor **Joanne B. Eicher**, *Regents' Professor, University of Minnesota*

Books in this provocative series seek to articulate the connections between culture and dress which is defined here in its broadest possible sense as any modification or supplement to the body. Interdisciplinary in approach, the series highlights the dialogue between identity and dress, cosmetics, coiffure, and body alterations as manifested in practices as varied as plastic surgery, tattooing, and ritual scarification. The series aims, in particular, to analyze the meaning of dress in relation to popular culture and gender issues and will include works grounded in anthropology, sociology, history, art history, literature, and folklore.

ISSN: 1360-466X

Previously published titles in the Series

Helen Bradley Foster, *"New Raiments of Self": African American Clothing in the Antebellum South*

Claudine Griggs, *S/he: Changing Sex and Changing Clothes*

Michaele Thurgood Haynes, *Dressing Up Debutantes: Pageantry and Glitz in Texas*

Anne Brydon and Sandra Niesson, *Consuming Fashion: Adorning the Transnational Body*

Dani Cavallaro and Alexandra Warwick, *Fashioning the Frame: Boundaries, Dress and the Body*

Judith Perani and Norma H. Wolff, *Cloth, Dress and Art Patronage in Africa*

Linda B. Arthur, *Religion, Dress and the Body*

Paul Jobling, *Fashion Spreads: Word and Image in Fashion Photography*

Fadwa El-Guindi, *Veil: Modesty, Privacy and Resistance*

Thomas S. Abler, *Hinterland Warriors and Military Dress: European Empires and Exotic Uniforms*

Linda Welters, *Folk Dress in Europe and Anatolia: Beliefs about Protection and Fertility*

Kim K. P. Johnson and Sharron J. Lennon, *Appearance and Power*

Barbara Burman, *The Culture of Sewing*

Annette Lynch, *Dress, Gender and Cultural Change*

Antonia Young, *Women Who Become Men*

David Muggleton, *Inside Subculture: The Postmodern Meaning of Style*

Nicola White, *Reconstructing Italian Fashion: America and the Development of the Italian Fashion Industry*

Brian J. McVeigh, *Wearing Ideology: The Uniformity of Self-Presentation in Japan*

Shaun Cole, *Don We Now Our Gay Apparel: Gay Men's Dress in the Twentieth Century*

Kate Ince, *Orlan: Millennial Female*

Nicola White and Ian Griffiths, *The Fashion Business: Theory, Practice, Image*

Ali Guy, Eileen Green and Maura Banim, *Through the Wardrobe: Women's Relationships with their Clothes*

Linda B. Arthur, *Undressing Religion: Commitment and Conversion from a Cross-Cultural Perspective*

William J. F. Keenan, *Dressed to Impress: Looking the Part*

Joanne Entwistle and Elizabeth Wilson, *Body Dressing*

Leigh Summers, *Bound to Please: A History of the Victorian Corset*

Paul Hodkinson, *Goth: Identity, Style and Subculture*

Sandra Niessen, Ann Marie Leshkowich and Carla Jones, *Re-Orienting Fashion: The Globalization of Asian Dress*

DRESS, BODY, CULTURE

Fashion Foundations
Early Writings on Fashion and Dress

Edited by

Kim K. P. Johnson, Susan J. Torntore
and Joanne B. Eicher

BERG

Oxford • New York

First published in 2003 by
Berg
Editorial offices:
1st Floor, Angel Court, 81 St Clements Street, Oxford, OX4 1AW, UK
838 Broadway, Third Floor, New York, NY 10003-4812, USA

© Kim K. P. Johnson, Susan J. Torntore and Joanne B. Eicher 2003

Berg is an imprint of Oxford International Publishers Ltd.

Library of Congress Cataloging-in-Publication Data

British Library Cataloguing-in-Publication Data
A catalogue record for this book is available from the British Library.

ISBN   1 85973 614 9 (Cloth)
       1 85973 619 X (Paper)

Typeset by JS Typesetting Ltd, Wellingborough, Northants.
Printed in the United Kingdom by Biddles Ltd, Guildford and King's Lynn.

"Fashions in all our gesterings,
Fashions in our attyre,
Which (as the wise have thoughte) do cum,
And go in circled gyre."

(*A Medicinall Morall*, Drant, 1566)

Contents

Acknowledgments   ix

Introduction   1

Part 1: Dressing the Body   5

1 Origins and Motives   15
       Of the Custom of Wearing Clothes
       Michel de Montaigne   15
       The Significance of Clothes *Sylvia H. Bliss*   18
       Dress *Alfred E. Crawley*   21
       Customs and Beliefs: Ceremonial
       Alfred R. Radcliffe-Brown   27
       Dress *Ruth Bendict*   29
       Costumes and Ideologies *Hilaire Hiler*
       and Meyer Hiler   34

2 Physical Connections between the Body and Dress   37
       The Psychology of Clothing
       George Van Ness Dearborn   37
       Microcosmus: An Essay Concerning Man and His
       Relation to the World *Hermann Lotze*   40
       Some Aspects of the Early Sense of Self
       G. Stanley Hall   43

3 Health Issues and Dress Reform   51
       Fashion in Deformity *William Henry Flower*   51
       The Science of Dress
       Ada S. Ballin   54
       The Reform Dress *Amelia Bloomer*   59
       The Development and Function of Clothing
       Knight Dunlap   63

Contents

Part 2: Fashioning Identity   69

4   Establishing Identity   73
        On Fashion *William Hazlitt*   73
        Let Us Have a National Costume *Mary E. Fry*   77
        The Psychology of Woman's Dress
        William I. Thomas   81

5   Appearance Management   85
        Remarks on the Psychology of Clothes
        Louis W. Flaccus   85
        Psychology of Dress *Grace Margaret Morton*   87

Part 3: The "F" Word   91

6   Fashion as Change   97
        Development in Dress *George H. Darwin*   97
        Badges and Costumes *Herbert Spencer*   100
        Fashion *Georg Simmel*   104
        Motivation in Fashion *Elizabeth Hurlock*   107
        Fashion *Edward Sapir*   112
        Some Conclusions *James Laver*   114

7   Predicting Fashion Change   119
        On the Nature of Fashion *Agnes Brooks Young*   119

8   Fashion as Collective and Consumer Behavior   125
        Fashion Movements *Herbert Blumer*   125
        Of the Influence of Custom and Fashion upon our
        Notions of Beauty and Deformity *Adam Smith*   127
        The Economic Theory of Woman's Dress
        Thorstein B. Veblen   129
        Dress as an Expression of Pecuniary Culture
        Thorstein B. Veblen   132
        A Psychological Analysis of Fashion Motivation
        Estelle de Young Barr   136

Chronological Annotated Bibliography (1575–1940)   141

Index   153

Acknowledgments

Joanne B. Eicher and Margaret P. Grindereng first developed the majority of this material as a graduate-level course at the University of Minnesota – finding readings that contributed to this present endeavor. Professor Grindereng then taught the first offerings of the course and we thank her for her contributions. Catherine Black, who was a student in one of those early courses and who has subsequently taught the course, generously provided biographical materials for several of the authors. We also acknowledge University of Minnesota graduate research assistants Jennifer Yurchisin and Theresa Winge for their diligent detective work. Jennifer spent long hours tracking down original copies of the readings to prepare the excerpts for scanning. Theresa persistently searched for biographical information and assisted in locating illustrations. Lori Rowell, graduate research assistant at Illinois State University, transposed the bibliography into American Psychological Association style. Lois Williams, copyright administrator at the University of Minnesota's Copyright Office handled all of the permissions for the reading excerpts and illustrations. Kathryn Earle and her editorial staff were instrumental in several ways, especially in encouraging the publication idea. Samantha Jackson deserves special thanks for her work scanning and formatting all of the original readings without which we would not have completed the manuscript. Sara Everett worked to help bring the manuscript to completion. Finally, we want to acknowledge all of the University of Minnesota graduate students who took this course and thoughtfully added suggestions for new readings and biographical information over the years, helping to shape our final effort. Kim Johnson and Joanne Eicher specifically want to thank Mary Ellen Roach-Higgins, who over the years provided inspiration and several early references regarding origins and motives from many disciplines.

Kim K. P. Johnson, St. Paul, MN
Susan J. Torntore, Normal, IL
Joanne B. Eicher, St. Paul, MN

Introduction

Fashion exists in many areas of life, not only in the way we dress, but also in many other areas such as food, home furnishings, and even our ways of thinking. Most often, however, dress becomes the focus when fashion arises as a topic of discussion, and the discussion frequently centers on clothing. Our view and definition of dress is one that is a more encompassing concept than focusing on clothing alone. Dressing the body includes many acts and products that serve as a nonverbal communication system. As we dress the body, we manipulate, modify, and supplement it with a wide range of products and artifacts. These acts and products allow us a means to present ourselves to others through the development of personal, social, and cultural identities. In this regard, we use the definition of dress developed by Eicher and Roach-Higgins (1992, p. 5) "as an assemblage of body modifications and/or supplements displayed by a person in communicating with other human beings." We are further interested in fashion because the word indicates that some dress practices end and others take their place.

As scholars involved in writing and teaching about the topic of fashion in dress, we found that current writers – whether scholars, students, or journalists – believe that interest in fashion is a recent one.[1] Some imply that they have discovered fashion's importance. The excerpts in this book illustrate, along with the appended bibliography, that the study of fashion and dress has been and still is widely conducted by individuals reflecting many disciplines. Consequently, in organizing and selecting excerpts for this book, we illustrate that 1) the study of dress and study of fashion have been of long interest and 2) authors associated with a variety of disciplines seek to understand the phenomenon of fashion in dress. Our selected articles come from English-language sources highlighting concepts that continue to have relevance to readers in the twenty-first century. Our selections have dress or fashion or both as a primary focus for analysis or argument. The authors we

---

1. This book spins off from a graduate level course for students interested in the study of dress using early writings about dress. Joanne B. Eicher and Margaret P. Grindereng initiated the course at the University of Minnesota in the early 1980s. It has been taught since then, focusing both on the chronological development of the ideas and concepts involved.

selected, among them philosophers, anthropologists, sociologists, psychologists, economists, feminists, and social activists, demonstrate their concern with fashion and its importance in understanding human behavior.

To facilitate appreciation of this material, and to be able to place it within a context for the reader, we provide overview statements that precede each section of the book. Our goal is to provide the reader with some context for the reading along with identifying the thesis of each article and preparing the reader for what is included. We choose to present a thematic organization of the authors' excerpts in contrast to a chronological presentation, selecting themes that continue to intrigue contemporary writers and researchers such as health issues, fashion change, and dress reform. We highlight some of the current concerns about the *meaning* of fashion in dress in order to understand behavior related to dressing the body. Our selections qualify as classic writings on fashion and dress, writings that are often cited in both popular and academic literature. We also include others that have been overlooked and perhaps with this exposure will be considered classics. Overall our selections may be looked upon as seminal works that include some paradigm shifts and major contributions to thinking about dress. We append a bibliography for readers interested in additional early writings on fashion in dress. This larger list of citations provides a brief perspective of the history of writings on dress, therefore, allowing some appreciation of the chronology in the development of ideas related to fashion and dress, from Montaigne in 1575 through two publications in 1940.

Several considerations guided our decisions about which readings to include in this collection. One of the themes reflected in our selections is that of defining fashion and dress. Our selections allow the reader to track through time the view of these concepts and to assess how closely the authors' definitions fit with ours. Another concern in choosing the selections was to illustrate the diversity of opinions about fashion in dress along with the diversity in the authors' backgrounds and interests. However, the selections come primarily from a social-science orientation, not an aesthetic or environmental orientation (among others) that could have been equally possible. The interdisciplinary nature of interest in the field of dress and fashion becomes clear in perusing the selections, for they illustrate that interest in fashion and dress has not been confined to a single discipline. Given the fact that our selections largely straddle the nineteenth and early twentieth centuries, another theme that runs through many of the excerpts is the assumption of social Darwinism. It has been said that no book, other than the Bible, has had a greater effect on society than Darwin's *On the Origin of Species* (Menton, 1994). The evolutionary explanations arising from Darwinism had a major impact on the thinking of the authors who write about dress after its introduction in the late 1800s. The feature of Darwinism most often cited by those who attempt to justify their moral and social views with "science" (evolution), is the concept of the "survival of the fittest." This application of Darwinian doctrine to human society and behavior is known as social Darwinism (Menton). George Darwin, the son of Charles Darwin, was one of the first writers to apply evolutionary theory to dress. Another feature of these articles is the opportunity for readers to reflect on the diversity of methods used to study fashion and dress reflected in these readings. The selections reflect armchair methodologies as well as early positivistic and interpretative approaches. In addition to making note of methodological approaches our selections allow the reader to trace the progression of the types of questions and concerns writers had about fashion and dress. From early concerns about origins and motives for dressing the body to concerns about health, the concerns of contemporary writers echo the issues our early writers addressed.

We chose the year 1940 as an arbitrary endpoint for our collection of early writings on dress. In our collection of excerpts we maintain the spelling, formatting, and references of the original publications. We have renumbered footnotes to facilitate reading and supplied references when authors supplied references at the end of each reading. Also included at the end of each article is a brief biographical note about the author(s). Much of this biographical information was obtained from encyclopedia entries (Grolier.com and Ency-clopediaBritannica On-line), university websites, and other publications by the authors. We used ellipses at the beginning of an excerpt to indicate that other material preceded the selection. Most of our collection is material in the public domain. For those few that are not, we sought copyright permission and where unsuccessful in our search, we are happy to acknowledge the copyright holder when identified.

References

Eicher, J. B. and Roach-Higgins, M. E. (1992). Definition and classification of dress: Implications for analysis of gender roles. In R. Barnes and J. B. Eicher (Eds). *Dress and gender: Making and meaning.* Oxford & New York: Berg.

Menton, D. (1994). The religion of nature: Social Darwinism. Retrieved October 1, 2002 from www.gennet.org/metro15.htm.

Part 1

Dressing the Body

Dressing the Body

This part of the book is divided into three chapters to provide various writers' views on the question of why we dress. The first chapter focuses on origins and motives for dress. The second looks at the physical experience of dressing the body: herein, writers begin to address the role of dress in establishing a sense of the physical self. The third chapter presents dress reform and health issues related to dress. Authors in this section of this book represent a range of backgrounds such as art, anthropology, philosophy, philology, medicine, psychology, and feminism.

In attempting to answer the question of origins, writers address what is the source, or the beginnings of dress. In addressing motives, authors concentrate on answering what causes a person to act or identifying the impulse(s) that stimulated action. In discerning the motive for the origins of dressing the body, the question usually asked is about what causes people to dress their bodies in a certain way. What explanations exist for why humans dressed their bodies? We present common theories and conjectures on why humans dress the body. In our view, writers, in asking why did the act of dress originate, searched for motives as an explanation. In dealing with origins of human behavior we must become involved with prehistory. Origins can't be known without actual archaeological, written, or oral history evidence. Generally, we lack these types of evidence for early peoples. Therefore, we contend that only speculations answer the questions of *how* dress originated and *why* dress originated.

In these excerpts several writers hypothesize that some acts of dressing the body originated with the motive of protecting the body. Our selections indicate suppositions or extrapolations to an earlier time with many writers basing their conjectures for the origins of dress on their contemporary views of a civilization that is inherent in a social-evolutionary or social-Darwinist perspective. A stated assumption of some of these authors is that we can learn something about the origins of dress by looking at what we see today and projecting backward. By making this a stated assumption, some of these authors recognize that this approach may not be accurate. Other authors do not clearly state this assumption but appear to us to be guided by it.

In textile and clothing courses and early textbooks, with a focus on the socio-cultural, historical, and socio-psychological aspects of dress, an early exercise is to speculate on the early origins and motives of dressing the body. Although we can continue speculating about origins and motives, as noted earlier we take the approach of Crawley (1912, see p. 21 of this volume) that the evidence we need in order to answer this question is lacking. What we have are some artifacts and much descriptive material. Speculations are more of a reflection of what we know or how we use materials than real knowledge of the actual origins and motives. However, there is value in acknowledging these early writers' views because this material presents us with the opportunity to realize that many ideas about dress and fashion are not new.

Origins and Motives

Michel de Montaigne (1575), as one of the earliest writers to reflect on dress, focuses on the very question of why humans wear clothing. In his essay, his use of the term clothing seems to be consistent with our use of the term dress. He attempts to explain why humans wear clothing, and why we have adopted these "borrowed means" (p. 224). Montaigne stated that "the naked state" (p. 225) is the natural condition and undressed humans, like all living things, did not need artificial protection against the effects of the physical environment. However, humans lost this protection when they started wearing clothes. In his essay, he asks whether nakedness is the original custom of human beings. Montaigne questions whether humans truly dress the body as a form of protection. His answer proposes custom as the main explanation for dressing the body. Montaigne's essay, presented in its entirety, reflects his interest in uncovering universal explanations and determining whether these explanations derive from natural or man-made laws. He took what can be labeled a Darwinist approach even though he wrote prior to the time of Darwin's theory of evolution. In questioning whether protection for environmental reasons was the original motive for dressing the body, his work is an early attempt at an explanation within a cultural perspective.

Sylvia Hortense Bliss (1916), in her attempt to construct a philosophy of clothing, also addresses the question of why humans wear clothes. Her answer spans two disciplinary perspectives – anthropology and psychoanalysis. She discusses the origins and functions of clothing from her contemporary standpoint four centuries after Montaigne. Although Bliss uses the terms clothing, costume, apparel, and dress interchangeably, she defines dress consistently with our preferred definition.

Bliss (1916) introduces the idea of humans as incomplete and unfinished beings compared to the rest of nature. She suggests that dress embodies and reflects unconscious or subconscious ideals and ideas. Rather than dress originating as custom, as both Montaigne (1575) and Crawley (1912) suggest, Bliss argues that the history of dress is a process of humans striving for the perfect "human costume" (p. 226). She proposes that this will be "fitting, natural, and characteristic as the exterior of fur and feathers for animal and bird" (p. 225). Unlike Darwin (1872), who interpreted a change in clothing as an evolutionary process in response to changing needs and functions, Bliss suggests that a change in clothing signifies a change in collective mental outlook. Her notion echoes the ideas of Carl Jung's collective unconscious[1] and Henri Bergson's creative evolution.[2]

Alfred E. Crawley's (1912) work was first published as an essay in an encyclopedia and later reprinted in a book, *Dress, Drinks and Drums*. In our excerpt he is also concerned with the origins of and motives for dressing the body. Crawley appears to use both the terms dress and clothing interchangeably, and in his analysis refers to a full definition of dress consistent with ours when he says "if dress be taken to include anything worn on the person, other than armor . . ." (p. 22). Our excerpt directly focuses on origins and motives, summarizing the existing hypotheses. He categorizes what he sees as the prevalent hypotheses into three distinct groups: the decorative element, the idea of concealment as related to modesty and sexual attraction, and the need for protection.

Crawley (1912) believes that since we have no direct evidence about the origins of dress, the reasons for origins remain as only speculations. He sees the main question as the process of invention, not the invention of dress. Our excerpt also presents his ideas that dress is a means for extending the body's capabilities and for allowing social display. In comparing clothing to a house in affording the same kind of environmental protection, he states that dress is "an extension of the passive area of a person" (p. 4), a "second skin" (p. 4) that allows people to not only to adapt their environment but to have mastery over it. Crawley uses an evolutionary model in his discussion. Dress comes from people adapting to their environment; he believes dress should be treated in the same way as weapons, machines, and tools. He expands

---

1. Psychiatrist Carl Jung (1965) introduced the concept of collective unconscious, which originates in the inherited structure of the brain, representing a form of the unconscious mind common to humankind as a whole. It includes memories, impressions, and impulses shared by all.

2. Creative evolution is a theory developed by French philosopher Henri Bergson (1911) to bring the elements of intuition, human intelligence, and unpredictability into the mechanistic theory of evolution. It would apply to the use of creativity in material culture settings.

the biological view of evolution and uses the religious and social significance of dress as a guide to include the psychological evolution of dress.

Crawley (1912) builds on the work of Lotze (1887), Hall (1898), and Spencer (1896), and provides an early anthropological approach to the study of dress. He sees dress as both an expression and extension of personality, and in this sense, then, explains how dress extends the capabilities of the body. Dress marks various biological and social grades in life, such as age, gender, and status. Dress, as a social form, is a social habit and becomes a direct affirmation of the personality and the state, expressing family, social movement and changing social roles, and government. He also extends the concept of dress as protection to include the psychic or psychological protection of dress used as an amulet, as protection from evil, the evil eye, and evil spirits. Crawley's work is an important development in the study of dress as a form of communication, as social display, and as social currency.

Alfred R. Radcliffe-Brown (1922) limits discussion of the origins and motives of dressing the body to a narrow view of dress as personal ornament. In this excerpt, drawn from a chapter in his book, he questions the meaning and social function of personal ornament. Radcliffe-Brown does not use the term dress or clothing in this discussion but discusses modifications made to the body along with supplements such as necklaces. His focus is dress. His hypothesis is that personal ornament is "a means by which the society acts upon, modifies, and regulates the sense of self in the individual" (p. 315). He provides two motives for the use of personal ornament – the desire for protection and the desire for display. "All ornament marks the relation of the individual to the society, and to forces/power in society to which he owes his well-being and happiness (p. 319)." He uses numerous observations and examples from his fieldwork as an anthropologist to talk about dress displaying dependence on society. When dressing the body, a person uses dress to mark and even highlight a position or place in society, making the person visible either temporarily or permanently. In addition to the concept of dress marking and displaying social value, Radcliffe-Brown, like Crawley (1912), believes dress offers protection from the meta-physical as well as the physical environment.

Ruth Benedict (1931), an anthropologist writing a definition of dress for the *Encyclopedia of the Social Sciences*, offers the view that we can know why people clothed themselves in the past by examining the present. She refers to this process of examining the present as conducting a comparative study of the "divergent behavior of now existing peoples" (p. 235). She outlines contemporary theories of origins and motives for dressing the body, such as originating from ideas of magic and protection, as protection against the rigors of climate, or as a means of sexual attraction. She discards one

popular theory – the notion of modesty as an instinct for expression in clothing. However, she states that all other theories of the origins of dress contain
"varied amounts of truth" (p. 236). Benedict uses the terms dress and clothing
interchangeably without defining them; her use is consistent with our use of
the term dress. In addition to summarizing the theories of the origins of
clothing, Benedict makes one major distinction between the dress of earlier
civilizations and modern dress. Whereas early dress was differentiated
geographically, she sees contemporary dress as differentiated in time, claiming
that the rise of fashion is a system of change that developed during the
Renaissance. Benedict hypothesizes that "this swift succession of styles will
maintain itself as a fixed characteristic of dress as a culture trait in our
civilization" (p. 237). In other words, fashion, as change in styles, is not
only a fixed characteristic of dress but also a cultural trait.

Hilaire Hiler and Meyer Hiler (1939), in their *Bibliography of Costume*,
provide the reader with a classification system of all of the theories explaining
or hypothesizing why humans dress the body. In developing their classification
system, they draw from sources in various fields of interest and study, such
as the fashion industry, ethnology, history, painting, theater, advertising, and
sociology. Hiler and Hiler contend that these theories – "the psychological
and social factors underlying all costume development." (p. iv) – explain the
development of dress around the world. Their use of the term costume relates
to Radcliffe-Brown's (1922) conceptualization of dress as limited to personal
ornament. Hiler and Hiler use the term costume to mean "dressing up"
(p. xii) or ornamenting and adorning the body in styles distinct from what
they refer to as "habitual" (p. xiii) clothing or the garments worn to protect
the body from the environment. This use of dress and costume is clearly different
from ours.

Physical Connections between the Body and Dress

George Van Ness Dearborn (1918) attempts to contribute to what he refers
to as the new science of clothing. Echoing the approach of Montaigne (1575),
Dearborn mounts an argument with a scientific approach about discovering
the laws underlying clothing behavior. He includes two parts to his mono-
graph – a physiological psychology of clothing and what he views as the
beginnings of an applied psychology of clothing. His use of the term clothing
is limited to styles of garments and is not inclusive. Our excerpt comes from
the section on the physiological psychology of clothing. Dearborn maintains
that "one's clothes are one of the important things that intervenes between
the individual personality and his environment and you understand that life
itself in a sense is a reaction of an individual to his environment" (p. 4).

Dearborn (1918) emphasizes that humans, in order to be "both more efficient and happy," need to be educated in how to dress "properly" (p. 1). The term, according to Dearborn, properly relates to how dress impacts the functions of the physical body, such as breathing, sweating, heart rate, movement of limbs and even digestive action, as well as to the psychological sense of comfort and well-being of the whole person. An important aspect of his applied psychology of clothing is his conclusion that "there can be no 'laws' social and much less official for scientifically clothing the population" (p. 69). In other words, science must apply itself to suggesting how individuals should dress rather than how an entire society should dress.

German philosopher Rudolf Hermann Lotze (1887), in his seminal essay, credits clothing as giving human beings sensations and feelings of existence. Dress, in contact with the surface of the physical body, can increase or facilitate feelings of the continuation of the person. In his own words, "the consciousness of our personal existence is prolonged into the extremities and surfaces of this foreign body and the consequence is feeling now an expansion of our proper self" (p. 592). In fact, dress or clothing, terms which Lotze uses synonymously and which refer only to garments, are tools to create self-consciousness, just as a stick held in the hand or the hands themselves are tools that extend the body. Our excerpt is part of his major work on the theory of knowledge and reality, in which he focused on humans and their relation to the world. This work, which began the study of dress and aware-ness of self, influenced several of his contemporaries including Hall (1898) and Spencer (1896), and subsequent scholars including Crawley (1912) and Bliss (1916), among many others.

G. Stanley Hall (1898) builds upon what he calls the concept of "Lotzean self-feeling" (p. 366), and looks at children to determine the development of the sense of self. He bases his presentation on data utilizing a questionnaire distributed to teachers and focused on their observations of children. He believes that mental growth progresses in evolutionary stages, and his present-ation outlines those stages. His main concern in this excerpt is psychological. His focus is on how humans develop physical self-consciousness. Using the terms dress and clothing interchangeably, Hall contends that dress and adornment are used to attract the attention of a child to its body. In other words, clothes consciousness facilitates body consciousness. One of the primary purposes of clothing for Hall is to get children on the correct develop-mental path. Hall suggests that clothing has a moral impact on children in that a change of dress can change a child's attitude and behaviors. Thus, how you dress a child is critical to the development of self. Hall offers a critique of Lotze (1887) by saying that Lotze's view about self-feeling as the purpose of clothing in childhood is too extreme. Hall instead posits that clothing on children can function to secure the attention and interest of others, that it is how clothing looks that counts, not how it feels. However, he does credit Lotze with showing that clothing is an integral part of self-consciousness.

Heath Issues and Dress Reform

As a physician and surgeon, William Henry Flower (1881) calls for dress reform but not as a women's issue. His book presents a history of what he calls deformities to the body in the name of fashion in both Western and non-Western settings. Flower contends that any body modification as result of dress, such as wearing tight corsets or fashionable shoes, deforms the natural body and as a result is an immoral act. He uses the term dress to include such body modifications as tattooing and corseting and is consistent with our use of the term. According to Flower, nature should be used as the standard of beauty, and dress reform, not fashion, is the way to preserve a civilized society.

Ada Ballin (1885) also focuses her concern on dress as it relates to health. She takes a human ecological approach in her book, taking into account humans and their near environment. She points out how some of the physical aspects or needs of the body, such as maintaining body temperature or ventilation, may be enhanced or inhibited by different body supplements. She recommends prescriptions for healthy dress, and proposes a "rational dress system" (p. 171) to maximize health and beauty. According to Ballin, this system must be fashionable as well as healthy or else it will not be successful. It is her objective to point out how clothing can be made healthy without being unfashionable. She contends that "sanitarians may preach forever without making a single convert, since women – especially women in Society – dread, and have reason to dread, ridicule, and they would endure tortures rather than appear unfashionable" (p. v). She uses the term dress as a synonym for clothing without a broader definition. Ballin, an early contributor to what she refers to as the science of dress, proposes practical applications as well as presenting the theories behind them.

One well-known solution to the calls for women's dress reform was the Bloomer costume, which was based on a pair of Turkish harem pants and a long, loose tunic. A common misconception about suffragist Amelia Bloomer's (1895) relationship to dress reform and the ensemble associated with her name is that she designed it and promoted it as part of the dress reform movement. However, as she herself explains in the excerpt taken from the biography written by her husband, Bloomer stopped wearing it eventually because it detracted from the real reform focus of her work, which was women's rights and suffrage. Bloomer wore the style of reform dress because she saw it as convenient for maintaining her busy lifestyle and because it fit within her philosophy.

Like Flower (1881) and Ballin (1885), Knight Dunlap (1928) also calls for dress reform, albeit forty years after the time-frame of what dress historians designate as the dress-reform movement, but his issue is not physical health. In the section on "the psychological problem of clothing" (p. 64), Dunlap discusses the problems of determining the motives for dressing the body. He concludes that the origins of clothing were in the human need for protection from "injurious and unpleasant agencies" (p. 69) such as insects. Ornaments and fashionable dress do not offer practical protection but instead confer status and communicate identity. While he differentiates clothing from ornament, Dunlap restricts his use of the term clothing to mean garments.

Dunlap (1928) contends that modesty evolved only once it became possible to indicate one's wealth and social status through dress. He also suggests that clothing developed along gender lines based on a practical basis of sexual selection. Men's clothing became practical to suit their economic needs and strength, and women's clothing developed along the lines of enhancing beauty. In his view, the clothing of his time period equalized sexual competition. Men and women of all status levels could look alike through their use of dress. This meant that a prostitute could be mistaken for a woman of society, and it is in this characteristic of dress that he finds a moral issue and calls for dress reform. "When we return to the primitive basis of clothing, as a means of protection and nothing more, we will have lost most of our problems of sexual morality . . ." (p. 78). Dunlap takes an unusual stance in wanting to return to the primitive state, rather than propounding the notion of social evolution and the trend to civilization.

References

Jung, C. G. (1965). *Memories, dreams, reflections.* (Rev. ed. A. Jaffé, ed.; R. & C. Winston, Trans.). New York: Vintage.

Bergson, H. (1911). *Creative evolution.* (A. Mitchell, Trans.). London: Macmillan; New York: H. Holt.

1

Origins and Motives

Of the Custom of Wearing Clothes *Michel de Montaigne*

Whatever I may be aiming at, I am obliged to force some barrier of custom: so carefully has she barred all our approaches I was considering within myself in this chilly season, whether the fashion of going about quite naked, in those lately discovered nations, is a fashion imposed by the warm temperature of the air, as we say of the Indians and the Moors, or whether it is the original custom of mankind. Inasmuch as all things under heaven, as the holy word

Figure 1.1 "If we had been born on condition of wearing farthingales and galligaskins . . ." Although Montaigne despairs about the lack of clothing worn by peasants in his countryside, in comparison, fashionable men of 1574 are no more covered in their lower extremities. From *History of British Costume* (p. 338), by J.R. Planché, 1847, London: C. Cox.

declares,[1] are subject to the same laws, men of understanding are wont, in considerations such as these, where we must distinguish the natural laws from those which have been invented, to have recourse to the general polity of the world, where there can be nothing counterfeit.

Now, all other creatures being fittingly provided with needle and thread, to maintain their being, it is really not to be believed that we alone should have been brought into the world in this defective and indigent state, in a state that cannot be maintained without foreign aid. So I hold that, as plants, trees, animals, all that lives, are by Nature equipped with sufficient covering to protect them against the injury of the weather,

> And therefore almost all Are covered either with hides, or else with shells,
> Or with the horny callus, or with bark, (LUCRETIUS.)

so were we; but, like those who with artificial light extinguish the light of day, we have extinguished our proper means with borrowed means. And it is easy to see that it is custom that makes impossible to us, what is not so: for among those nations that have no knowledge of clothes, there are some that dwell in much the same climate as we do; and moreover, the most delicate parts of us are those which are always uncovered, the eyes, the mouth, the nose, the ears; in the case of our peasants, as with our ancestors, the pectoral and ventral parts. If we had been born on condition of wearing farthingales and galligaskins, I make no doubt but that Nature would have armed with a thicker skin what she has exposed to the battery of the seasons, as she has done the finger-ends and the soles of the feet.

Why does this seem hard to believe? Between my habit of clothing and that of a peasant of my country-side there is a much greater distance than between his and that of a man who is clothed only in his skin.

How many men, especially in Turkey, go naked as a matter of religion! Somebody or other asked one of our beggars whom he saw in his shirt in the depth of winter, as merry as a grig and feeling the cold as little as many a man who is muffled up to the ears in sable, how he could patiently bear it. "And you, sir, he replied, you have your face uncovered; now, I am all face." The Italians tell a tale of, I think, the Duke of Florence's fool, that his master asking him how, being so poorly clad, he could bear the cold, which he himself was hardly able to do: "Follow my recipe, he replied, and pile on all the garments you have, like me, and you will feel the cold no more than I do." King Massinissa could not be induced, even in his extreme old age, to go with his head covered, were it ever so cold, stormy or rainy. The same is told of the Emperor Severus.

1. Ecclesiastes ix. 2,3.

In the battles fought between the Egyptians and the Persians, Herodotus says that both he and others remarked that, of those who were left dead on the field, the skulls of the Egyptians were without comparison harder than those of the Persians, by reason that the latter always have their heads covered, first with biggins and afterwards with turbans, and the former are shaven from infancy and uncovered.

And King Agesilaus observed the habit, until his decrepitude, of wearing the same clothing in winter as in summer. Caesar, says Suetonius, always marched at the head of his army, and most often on foot, bareheaded, whether in sunshine or rain; and the same is said of Hannibal;

Bareheaded then he braved the raging storm. (SILIUS ITALICUS.)

A Venetian, who had long resided in the kingdom of Pegu, and has but lately returned from thence, writes that both the men and women of that country always go barefoot, even on horseback, the rest of their body being clothed.

And Plato gives this wonderful advice, that, to keep the whole body in health, we should give the feet and head no covering but that which Nature has provided. The man who, following our King, was chosen King of Poland,[2] and who is indeed one of the greatest princes of our age, never wears gloves, nor does he change, however severe the weather in winter, the bonnet he wears indoors. Just as I cannot go loose and unbuttoned, the labourers round about here would feel fettered if they had to button up. Varro contends that, when it was ordained that we should uncover in presence of the gods or the magistracy, it was rather for our health's sake, and to harden us against the inclemency of the weather, than upon the account of reverence.

Source   Excerpted from de Montaigne, M. (1927). *The essays of Montaigne.* (Vol 1). London: Oxford University Press. (Original work published 1575)

Biographical note   Michel de Montaigne (1533–1592) was a French essayist, a widely read writer of the French Renaissance, who lived in Bordeaux. He is generally acknowledged as the inventor of the personal or familiar essay as a modern literary genre. This reading was drawn from what is considered to be his best-known work, a collection of essays published in three volumes between 1580 and 1588, and first translated into English in 1603.

✽ ✽ ✽

2. Henri III and Stephen Bathori

The Significance of Clothes *Sylvia H. Bliss*

. . . Discriminating and applicable though these theories may be it is obvious that no one of them adequately accounts for the fact of clothing nor sufficiently explains its complexity and variety. It may be, as one writer suggests, that the ancient Britons painted the body with earthy pigments to check the cooling effect of free evaporation from the skin; that the Andaman Islanders plaster themselves thickly with mud in order to resist the attacks of insects; the skin mantle of the Fuegian, shifted to meet the varying winds, and the elaborately fitted fur garments of the Eskimo, are obviously worn in deference to rigorous climate; the gourd or sling of certain South American tribes probably serves as a protection from injury, and the exceedingly small pearl-decorated apron of the Kafir belle is doubtless worn as a means of attraction; vanity, aesthetic feeling, the desire for distinction and the motive of comfort play their part. But as the primitive clothing impulse manifests itself in such varied forms we are justified in retreating beyond these partial hypotheses to one more profound and fundamental which underlies and includes them all.

Too great stress must not be laid on the factor of use, on an assumed end determining the particular form taken by the primitive impulse to decorate or clothe the body. The doctrine of use as a factor in evolution finds less favor than formerly. In the language of Professor William Patten of Dartmouth College, "The use made of an organ can not be the cause of its origin, for the organ must be present in the first place, in some form or other, before any use can be made of it:" and while to-day we find man by reason of his acquired equipment of reason and foresight working toward definitely conceived ends, it is hardly reasonable to attribute to the primitive creature at the outset of the human career clearly defined motives which determined his acts. As has been pointed out by the naturalists Geddes and Thompson, human nature can not be rightly understood apart from the biological approach, and even in a matter apparently so far removed from the natural as that of clothing there will be found many analogies to zoölogical and biological facts. Primitive psychological attitudes from what has been termed physiological thought and the instinctive inner urge prompting the acts of primitive man may be not inaptly compared to those special internal conditions which biologists recognize as determining local growths, organs and structure, lower down in the scale of life.

In order adequately to frame a philosophy of clothes it is necessary to view as clearly as possible man's place in nature. Though there are now on earth only isolated examples of hairy men it is probable that the primitive human being and certainly his precursor were covered with hair. We may or may not accept the Darwinian conclusion that the loss of our coat of hair was due to aesthetic reasons, "the members of one sex having chosen as mates those of the other who were least hairy" but the fact remains that man, as Carlyle said, is by nature a naked animal. Moreover he is, broadly speaking, the only naked animal. In the world of living things are displayed fur, feathers, thickened and colored hide, scales, various armors, and integuments, for the tree bark and for all plant forms fitness and beauty of investiture. Man alone is left with an incomplete exterior. His position in nature is anomalous. All other creatures are finished and complete, clothed and with instinct sufficient to form themselves an abode which remains unaltered with the passing of the ages. Man alone must supplement nature. He has progressed by reason of his incompleteness and to what extent his initial advance was due to the lack of a satisfactory and fitting exterior is matter for conjecture. The gods left man naked in order that he might clothe himself: unfinished that he might indefinitely continue the process of development.

Underlying all the various motives which apparently lead man to paint, tattoo, decorate and protect the body is the fundamental feeling of incompleteness, of dissatisfaction with self as it is, and clothing in its origin and subsequent development is the result of his attempt to remedy the deficiency, to replace what he has lost. The covering and ornament which human beings supply for the body stand in lieu of fur, feathers, and all the varied exteriors found in lower nature and further, serve like ends of protection and adornment. The fact of the reputed complete nakedness of certain peoples does not militate against this theory of the primary reason for clothing. While individuals may be entirely nude it is said that in no tribe do all the members remain constantly as nature left them. Study of "our contemporary ancestors" discloses, it is probable, most of the forms of adornment and body covering used by prehistoric man – complicated in many instances by contact of the savages with civilized races – and as might be expected there are peoples in whom the clothing impulse has not developed, or but feebly, going no farther than paint, the mutilation of some organ or the wearing of a necklace or belt . . .

Man's place in nature must be still further defined if we are to appreciate to the full the significance of clothing. Humanity appears to be a continuation of the main stem of life of which all lower forms are the branches. They diverged from the central stem, advanced a pace and became what Nietzsche would term the goals of nature, plant, insect, animal and bird – man, according to the German philosopher's thought, being not a goal but a bridge. The life which was to become human continued to advance though divested of many possibilities. It is not necessary to accept all the implications of Bergson's philosophy in order to make use of his pregnant idea that life, evolving in the direction of man has abandoned many things by the way.

Tendencies which were incompatible with the main trend of life were dropped and set up a subordinate line of development. Applying this conception to the matter in hand we may say that man has left far behind the possibility of a furred or feathered exterior, of blossoms, thorns, horns, tails, and countless other structures and appendages displayed by lower forms of life, plant and animal. It may be said further – and here is the crucial point in our philosophy of clothes – that these structures, appendages and ornaments which are characteristic of life other than human, survive in man as subconscious dispositions which at various times in the world's history, some in one race and some in another, are embodied in his dress. Actual physical survivals of lower forms of life appear during the development of the human fetus. Certain of these disappear, others are modified to form working parts of the organism, while occasionally one persists as an atrophied structure in the fully developed human being. In the light of these facts we are warranted in assuming the presence of corresponding mental survivals. The variety and vagary of garb are thus not due to mere whim and vagary of the human mind. Man is the epitome of all tendencies and the reason for the complexity of his clothing impulse may be found in the complexity of his mental inheritance which includes all that he has lost physically on the way to man. There is scarcely a covering in nature that has not been utilized or imitated in human apparel; there can hardly be found a protuberance or appendage that may not have served as the prototype for some form of human mutilation or adornment. Fur serves both savage and civilized man. Certain tribes of the Amazon basin fix a covering of feathers on their bodies, daubed with a sticky substance; other tribes insert feathers in perforations in the cheek or nasal septum, while feathers as adornment, especially of the head are found the world over and not least in modern civilized nations. There are striking simulations of horns, notably the head-dress of some African tribes, and in England what has been called "the preposterous horned head-dress" of the reign of Henry V the student of costume will come upon many an arresting likeness of coronet, cockade, neck ruff, stock, and frill, plume, sash, and train, to natural organic characteristics of other creatures and it is interesting to note in passing that a caricature of the date of 1786, entitled "Modern Elegance," shows two women wearing the Bouffon, an exaggerated neckerchief of cambric, and above them the figure of a Pouter pigeon with characteristically inflated oesophagus.

Perhaps the most striking example of physiological habit surviving in man as a mental tendency is that of the tail. This appendage has been so often simulated that it has given rise to the fable of men with tails and even our modern sash and train may, without stretch of the imagination, be referred to a like lowly origin. The student of savage costume comes again and again upon instances of this addition to man's natural equipment and while the claim may be made that this widespread habit is due to imitation of animals it may with greater reasonableness be attributed to the subconscious reminiscence of an actual tail. This view is strengthened by the fact that the tail-like ornament is often worn on the front of the body and quite naturally the conclusion is reached that the various forms of the fig leaf, apron and clout may be included in the same category. The tail being one of the most recent of our losses, physical vestiges of this appendage occasionally, it is said, persisting in man, the impulse to thus supplement the body is strong. Deeper than the ends which they serve is the reason for all forms of apparel.

Source Excerpted from Bliss, S.H. (1916). The significance of clothes. *American Journal of Psychology, 27,* 217–226.

Biographical note Sylvia Hortense Bliss (1870–1963) is described as a writer, accomplished musician, and amateur botanist. She studied music in Iowa and at Syracuse University. She taught piano lessons and was a church organist. She sought medical treatment for a speech handicap with Boston neurologists Dr. Morton Prince and Dr. James Putnam and it was during this period (1909–1918) that she researched and published articles in the *American Journal of Psychology* and the *Journal of Abnormal Psychology* on subjects that interested her as a layperson.

* * *

Dress *Alfred E. Crawley*

DRESS – An analysis of the relations of man's clothing with his development in social evolution will naturally be chiefly concerned with psychological categories. When once instituted, for whatever reasons or by whatever process, dress became a source of psychical reactions, often complex, to a greater extent (owing to its more intimate connexion with personality) than any other material product of intelligence. Some outline of the historical development of dress will be suggested, rather than drawn, as a guide to the main inquiry. The practical or, if one may use the term, the biological uses and meaning of dress, are simple enough and agreed upon. These form the first state of the material to be employed by the social consciousness. Its secondary states are a subject in themselves . . .

Origins – The primary significance of dress becomes a difficult question as soon as we pass from the institution in being to its earliest stages and its origin. For speculation alone is possible when dealing with the genesis of dress. Its conclusions will be probable, in proportion as they satisfactorily bridge the gulf between the natural and the artificial stages of human evolution. The information supplied by those of the latter that are presumably nearest to the natural state, to *Protanthropus,* is not in itself a key to the origin of clothing, but, on the other hand, the mere analogy of animal-life is still less helpful . . .

It may serve, however, to point by contrast the actual continuity of the natural and the artificial stages, the physical and the psychical stages, of our evolution. If we say that man is the only animal that uses an artificial covering for the body, we are apt to forget that even when clothed he is subject to the same environmental influences as in the ages before dress. Again, there is no hint that the approach of a glacial epoch inaugurated the invention of dress. But it is an established fact that the survivors of immigrants to changed conditions of climate and geological environment become physically adapted by some means of interaction and in certain directions of structure, which are just coming to be recognized . . . The most obvious of these natural adaptations, physiologically produced, to the environment is pigmentation. The skin of man is graded in colour from the Equator to the Pole. The deeper pigmentation of the tropical skin is a protection against the actinic rays of the sun; the blondness of northern races, like the white colour of Arctic animals, retains the heat of the body.

If we followed the analogy of the animal, we should have to take into account the fact that a mechanical intelligence enables it to obviate certain disadvantages of its natural covering. The animal never exposes itself unnecessarily; its work, in the case of the larger animals, is done at night, not in the glare of the sun. Automatically it acquires an artificial covering in the form of shelter. If man in a natural state followed a similar principle, he would be at no more disadvantage than is the animal. A similar argument applies to the other use mentioned above, namely, sexual decoration. What these considerations suggest is that man was not forced by necessity to invent. The reason is at once deeper and simpler. Again, we get the conclusion that one primary use and meaning of dress is not so much to provide an adaptation to a climate as to enable man to be superior to weather; in other words, to enable him to move and be active in circumstances where animals seek shelter. The principle is implicit in the frequent proverbial comparison of clothing to a house.

Dress, in fact, as a secondary human character, must be treated, as regards its origins, in the same way as human weapons, tools, and machines. Dress increases the static resisting power of the surface of the body, just as tools increase the dynamic capacity of the limbs. It is an extension (and thereby an intension) of the passive area of the person, just as a tool is of the active mechanism of the arm. It is a second skin, as the other is a second hand. Further, if we take an inclusive view of evolution, admitting no break between the natural and the artificial, but regarding the latter as a sequence to the former, we shall be in a position to accept indications that both stages, and not the former only, are subject to the operation of the same mechanical laws, and show (with the necessary limitations) similar results. These laws belong to the interaction of the organism and the environment, and the results are found in what is called adaptation, an optimum of equilibrium, a balanced interaction, between the two . . . The selective process has not been conscious, but neither has it been accidental. It is the result of law. Equally unconscious in its first stages was the adaptation of dress to temperature. This brings us no nearer to the origins of dress, though it clears the ground. Still further to simplify speculation, we may notice some prevalent hypotheses on the subject. Dress being a covering, it assumes, when instituted, all the applicable meanings which the idea of covering involves. But it by no means follows that all of these, or even any, were responsible for its original institution.

There is, first, the hypothesis that clothing originated in *the decorative impulse*. This has the merit of providing a cause which could operate through unconscious intelligence, automatic feeling . . .

. . . It is in accordance with the rule among animals that among primitive peoples the male sex chiefly assumes decoration. Ornaments among the Indians of Guiana are more worn by men than by women. The stock ornamentation is paint; scented oils are used as vehicles . . .

But this analogy [the male sex . . .] is not to be pressed, though it is sound as far as it goes. It applies, that is, up to a certain point in social evolution. Beyond that point the balance inclines the other way, and for the last five hundred years of European civilization decorative dress has been confined to women . . .

In practical investigation it is difficult, as Ratzel[1] observes, to say "where clothing ends and ornament begins," or, on the previous hypothesis, where clothing springs out of ornament. Since either may obviously develop into the other when both are instituted, it is idle to examine such cases. Cases where one or the other is absolutely unknown might serve, but there are no examples of this. If an instance, moreover, of the presence of clothing and entire absence of ornament were observed, it would be impossible to argue that clothing cannot be subject to the decorative impulse. In any case, there is the self-feeling, satisfaction in individuality, to be reckoned with, for the impulse to finery is only one phase of it.

---

1. F. Ratzel, *History of Mankind* (1896–1898), i, 93–94.

The supporters of the ornamentation hypothesis of the origin of dress have an apparently strong argument in the Brazilians and the Central Australians. These recently studied peoples possess no clothing in the ordinary sense of the term. But they wear ornament, and on special occasions a great deal of it. Brazilian men wear a string round the lower abdomen, the women a strip of bark-cloth along the perineum, tied to a similar abdominal thread. This is sometimes varied by a small decorative enlargement. The Central Australian man wears a waist-string, to which is tied a pubic tassel. Corresponding to the last in the case of the women is a very small apron. Leaving the waist-string out of account, we have remaining the question of the erogenous centre. In both the decoration hypothesis and the concealment hypothesis this centre is the focus of speculation. If the Australian tassel of the male sex and the leaf-like enlargement of the Brazilian woman's perineal thread are considered superficially, they may appear to be, if not ornaments, at least attractions. But if this be granted, it does not follow that we have here the first application of the idea of dress. It would be impossible to make out a case to prove that these appurtenances can ever have satisfied the idea of *concealment,* as on the next hypothesis is assumed. This hypothesis is to the effect that male jealousy instituted clothing for married women . . .

. . . The general connexion between modesty and dress is a subject of little importance, except in so far as it has involved the creation of false modesty, both individually and socially. Modesty where there is dress, tends to be concentrated upon it mechanically. When clothing is once established, the growth of the conception of women as property emphasizes its importance, and increases the anatomical modesty of women. Waitz held that male jealousy is the primary origin of clothing, and therefore of modesty. Diderot had held this view. Often married women alone are clothed. It is as if before marriage a woman was free and naked; after marriage, clothed and a slave.

But the fact of dress serving as concealment involved the possibility of *attraction by mystery.* Even when other emotions than modesty, emphasized by male jealousy, intervene, they may work together for sexual attraction . . .

Finally, there is the *protection-hypothesis.* Sudden falls in the temperature, rains and winds and burning sunshine, the danger of injuring the feet and the skin of the body generally when in the forest, and the need of body-armour against the attacks of insects and of dangerous animals seem obvious reasons for the invention of dress. But they do not explain the process of invention, which is the main problem. The cloak, the skirt, the apron, cannot have been invented in answer to a need, directly, without any stages. The invention of cloth was first necessary, and this was suggested by some natural covering. The only line of development which seems possible is from protective ligatures. There are numerous facts which apparently point to such an origin of clothing. One of the most characteristic 'ornaments' of savages all over the world is the armlet. It is quite probable that this has an independent origin in the decorative impulse, like the necklace. But here and there we find bands worn round the ankles, knees, wrists, and elbows, the object of which is clearly to protect the sinews and muscles from strains. The pain of a strained muscle being eased by the grip of the hand, the suggestion of an artificial grip might naturally follow, and a system of ligatures would be the result . . .

Wild peoples, in fact, understand quite well the limitations and the capacity of the human organism in respect to the environment. We may credit them with an adequate system of supplying natural deficiencies, and of assisting natural advantages also . . .

. . . Now, the great majority of the lowest peoples known wear no clothes. Shelter is used instead. But there is very commonly a waist-string, and it is more used by men than by women. We assume that the girdle is the point of departure for the evolution of dress, and the mechanism of that departure will be presently discussed. But for the origin of body-clothing it is necessary to find the origin of the girdle. The civilized idea of a girdle is to bind up a skirt or trousers. This is certainly not its object among the earliest peoples, who have nothing to tie up. It might be supposed that the original purpose of the girdle was that of the abdominal belt, useful both as a muscle-ligature and to alleviate the pangs of hunger. But the earliest girdles are merely strings, and string is useless for such purposes. String, moreover, made of grass or vegetable fibre, or animal sinew or human hair, is an earlier invention than the bandage. Its first form was actually natural, the pliant bough or stem . . .

. . . The waist-string, therefore, being earlier than clothing proper, and being, as we have suggested, the point of departure for the wearing of coverings, we have next to examine the mechanism of the connexion between them. The use of the string as a holder being given, it would serve not only as a pocket, but as a suspender for leaves or bunches of grass, if for any reason these were required. The point to be emphasized here is that the presence of a suspender would suggest the suspension and therefore the regular use of articles for which there had been no original demand . . .

It is unnecessary to enter upon a description of the various zones of the body which require protection, such as the spine at the neck and in the small of the back, against sun and cold, or the mucous membranes of the perineal region, against insects. The use of clothing of certain textures and colours to maintain a layer of air about the skin at a temperature adapted to that of the body, and to neutralize those rays of light which are deleterious to the nervous system and destructive of protoplasm, is also out of place here. We may note, however, that by unconscious selection the evolution of dress has probably followed a thoroughly hygienic course. But no principles of such hygiene, except the very simplest, can have occurred to primitive man. One of the simplest, however, we way admit for tropical races – the use of a protection against insects. The perineal region is most subject to their attacks when man is naked, owing to the sebaceous character of the surface and its relatively higher temperature. These facts, no doubt, more than anything else, are the explanation of primitive habits of depilation. But depilation is not a complete protection. Something positive is required. The use of bunches of grass or leaves is natural and inevitable, as soon as there is something to hold them, namely, the waist-string. A parallel method is the use of a second string depending from the waist-string in front and behind, and passing between the legs. The Brazilian strip of bast used by women, and the red thread which takes its place in the Trumai tribe, though "they attract attention like ornaments instead of drawing attention away," yet, as Von den Steinen[2] also satisfied himself, provide a protection against insects, a serious pest in the forests of Brazil. These inter-crural strings protect the mucous membrane, without, however, concealing the parts, as do leaves and grass. In the present connexion their chief interest is the use made of the waist-string. When cloth was invented, the first form of the loin-cloth was an extension of the inter-crural thread . . .

. . . The protection-hypothesis of the origin of dress may thus be adopted, if we qualify it by a scheme of development as suggested above. When once instituted as a custom, the wearing of leaves or bark-cloth upon the abdominal region served to focus various psychical reactions. One of the earliest of these was the impulse to emphasize the primary sexual characters. It is an impulse shown among the great majority of early races in their observances at the attainment of puberty, and it is, as a rule, at that period that sexual dress or ornament is assumed. Among civilized peoples, in the Middle Ages and in modern times, the impulse is well marked by various fashions – the phallocrypt and the tail of the savage having their European analogues. A less direct but even more constant instance of the same recognition is the assigning of the skirt to women as the more sedentary, and trousers to men as the more active sex. The suggestion sometimes met with, that the skirt is an adaptation for sexual protection, need only be mentioned to be dismissed. The Central Australian pubic tassel and similar appendages will here find significance, but it is improbable that such accentuation was their original purpose. Once instituted for protection, the other ideas followed. Another of these, which

---

2. K. von den Steinen, *Unter den Naturvölkern Zentral-Brasiliens* (Berlin 1894), pp. 190f. For other protective coverings for the organs against insects, see Wilken-Pletye, Handleiding voor de vergelijkende Vokenkunde van Nederlandsch Nederlandscb-Indiē (Leyden 1893), pp. 37–38.

at once received an artificial focus, was the emotion of modesty. It has been observed among the higher animals that the female by various postures guards the sexual centres from the undesired advances of the male. The assumption of a waist-cloth does not actually serve the same purpose, but it constitutes a permanent psychical suggestion of inviolability. Similarly, the use of any appendage or covering involves the possibility of attraction, either by mere notification, by the addition of decoration, or, later, by the suggestion of mystery. Further than this, speculation as to origins need not be carried. The various forms and fashions of dress, and the customs connected with it, will supply examples of the material as well as of the psychological evolution of the subject.

. . . In spite of the underlying similarity of principles, universally found, dress more than any external feature distinguishes race from race and tribe from tribe. While distinguishing a social unit it emphasizes its internal solidarity. In this latter sphere there is, again, room for individual distinction . . .

Source Excerpted from Crawley, A.E. (1912). Dress. *Encyclopedia of religion and ethics* (Vol. 5, pp. 40–72). New York: Charles Scribner's Sons.

Biographical note Alfred Ernest Crawley (1869–1924) was a British social anthropologist. He was a Fellow of the Sociological Society and an Examiner to the University of London. He also wrote *The Mystic Rose* (1902), which contained research on "primitive" and "traditional" societies, such as magical and religious practices.

❊ ❊ ❊

Customs and Beliefs: Ceremonial
Alfred R. Radcliffe-Brown

We may now return to the question of the meaning of personal ornament in general. It is a commonplace of psychology that the development of the sense of self is closely connected with the perception of one's own body. It is also generally recognized that the development of the moral and social sentiments in man is dependent upon the development of self-consciousness, of the sense of self. These two important principles will help us to appreciate the hypothesis to which the discussion has now led, that in the Andamans the customary regulation of personal ornament is a means by which the society acts upon, modifies, and regulates the sense of self in the individual.

There are three methods of ornamenting the body in the Andamans, (1) by scarification, (2) by painting, and (3) by the putting on of ornaments.

The natives give two reasons for the custom of scarification, that it improves the personal appearance and that it makes the boy or girl grow up strong.

Both these mean that scarification gives or marks an added value. The explanation of the rite would therefore seem to be that it marks the passage from childhood to manhood and is a means by which the society bestows upon the individual that power, or social value, which is possessed by the adult but not by the child. The individual is made to feel that his value – his strength and the qualities of which he may be proud – is not his by nature but is received by him from the society to which he is admitted. The scars on his body are the visible marks of his admission. The individual is proud or vain of the scars which are the mark of his manhood, and thus the society makes use of the very powerful sentiment of personal vanity to strengthen the social sentiments.

Turning now to the painting of the body, we have seen that the pattern of white clay serves to make both the painted individual and those who see him feel his social value, and we have seen that this interpretation explains the occasions on which such painting is used. To complete the argument it is necessary to consider the occasions on which the use of white clay is forbidden.

Those to whom this prohibition applies are (1) a youth or girl who is aka-op, i.e., who is abstaining from certain foods during the initation period, (2) a mourner, (3) a homicide during the period the isolation, and (4) a person who is ill. All these persons are excluded from full participation in the active social life, and therefore the social value of each of them is diminished. It would obviously be wrong for a person in such a condition to express by decorating himself a social value that he did not at the time possess . . . All ornament in some way marks the relation of the individual to the society and to that force or power in society to which he owes his well-being and happiness. When painting or ornament is used to give protection, it is, as we have seen, the protective power of the society itself that is appealed to, and what is expressed is the dependence of the individual on the society. When ornament or paint is used for display it is again the dependence on the society that is expressed, though in a different way and on occasions of a different kind. We have seen that scarification is also a means of marking the dependence of the individual on the society, and it is very important to note that the Andamanese sometimes explain it as due to the desire for display and sometimes to the need of protection (enabling the child to grow strong and so avoid the dangers of sickness), showing very clearly that there is some intimate connection between these two motives, or at any rate that one and the same method of ornamentation can satisfy both. There is one further example of red paint, which is combined with the pattern of white clay for purposes of display, and is also constantly used in many ways as affording protection.

We are thus brought to the final conclusion that the scarification and painting of the body and the wearing of most if not all the customary ornaments are rites which have the function of marking the fact that the individual is in a particular permanent or temporary relation to that power in the society and in all things that affect social life, the notion of which we have seen to underlie so much of the Andaman ceremonial.

... In the various methods of ornamenting the body the two chief motives that we have considered are so combined that they can hardly be estimated separately, and it is this mingling of motives that has led us to the final understanding of the meaning and social function of bodily ornament. Each of the different kinds of ornament serves to make manifest the existence of some special relation between the individual and the society, and therefore of some special relation between him and that system of powers on which the welfare of the society and of the individual depends. One of the most important aspects of the relation of the individual to the society is his dependence upon it for his safety and well-being and this is revealed in all painting and ornament worn for protection. But the society not only protects the individual from danger; it is the direct source of his well-being; and this makes itself felt in the customary regulation by which the use of the more important ornaments used for display is confined to occasions on which it is quite clear that his happiness is directly due to the society, such as a dance or feast. Thus the customs relating to the ornamentation of the body are of the kind that I have here called ceremonial. They are the means by which the society exercises on appropriate occasions some of the important social sentiments, thereby maintaining them at the necessary degree of energy required to maintain the social cohesion ...

Source Excerpted from Radcliffe-Brown, A. R. (1922). The Andaman Islanders. Cambridge: Cambridge University Press.

Biographical note Sir Alfred Reginald Radcliffe-Brown (1881–1955) was a leading British social anthropologist. He conducted numerous ethnological studies in Africa, Australia, and North America. The featured reading is drawn from his fieldwork among the people of Andaman Islands of Australia. He is a functional anthropologist. A major contribution was his examination of behavioral patterns and institutions of a social system in terms of how they functioned. His goal was a science of society that would formulate laws, explaining how social systems operated.

* * *

Dress *Ruth Benedict*

For the history of dress there are roughly four fields of study: prehuman behavior, archaeology, primitive peoples and modem civilized conditions.

The study of animal behavior emphasizes two facts regarding the origin of clothing. In the first place, human dress, in so far as it is for protection against the elements, has no continuity with any prehuman behavior. Animals in frigid climates grow warm coats, which are transmitted to their offspring by heredity. The opposite technique of invention and traditionally transmitted processes does not occur except in man. In the second place, observation of the higher apes has emphasized the prehuman roots of clothing as self-decoration. Köhler describes the naïve delight of chimpanzees in hanging objects about their bodies and trotting about to display them.

Archaeology reveals nothing about the history of dress until the upper palaeolithic era – which is far removed from earliest man. Clothing is necessarily of perishable materials, but even ornaments of animal teeth, ivory and shells begin to appear only in the Aurignacian period at the same level at which is found the characteristic palaeolithic development of mural drawing and engraving. From this period date also the characteristically distorted nude figurines of the female form, some of which are wearing bracelets although they are not represented with any other clothing. It is obvious, however, that the distortion of these female figurines is in the direction of fertility symbols, and their nudity furnishes no information as to women's daily wear in the Aurignacian period except that bracelets were worn at this period.

The reasons that have led man to clothe himself can therefore be studied chiefly from a comparison of the divergent behavior of now existing peoples. There is a strong association in western civilization between dress and the covering of the sex organs, but most of the literature concerning the origin of clothing has directed its array of facts to demolish the assumption of the primacy of this connection and to point out that dress did not have its origin in a specific instinct of modesty focused on the organs of reproduction.

It is obvious from any study of primitive clothing that this particular function of dress has very often been unknown in other cultures. The habit of complete nudity has a wide distribution in the tropical regions of South America, Melanesia and Africa. In some cases both men and women are habitually naked, in others only the men, in still others only the women. Even outside of tropical regions habitual nudity is widespread, although a skin may be thrown over the shoulders for protection. Such regions are the Great Basin in North America, California and Australia. Even in arctic regions, where well tailored clothing is universal, the conventions are often such that both men and women are habituated to indoor nudity like all people so habituated exhibit no shame in uncovering. Nansen describes the inter-crural cord of the east coast of Greenland, the sole covering of the natives when indoors, as being "so extremely small as to make it practically invisible to the stranger's inexperienced eye" (*Paaski over Grönland*, Christiania 1890,

Tr. by H.M. Gepp as *The First Crossing of Greenland*, 2 vols., London 1890, vol. i, p. 338–39, vol. ii, p. 277–78).

In more extreme instances that may be brought to bear against this theory of the origin of clothing in an instinct of modesty the very nature of the coverings themselves is the point of the argument. The codpiece which was worn in Europe about 1450 and the custom of the men of certain Papuan tribes who squeeze their members into the opening of a gourd are indicative of the exhibitionist nature of certain forms of dress. Many observers in many parts of the world have commented on the fact that the most obvious function of the genital coverings was to attract attention rather than to divert it.

It is possible therefore to discard the notion that there is a human instinct of modesty that expresses itself in clothing. Modesty is a conditioned reflex and has its roots in the fashion of dress to which any group is accustomed. It is therefore to be expected that, given certain turns of fashion, other regions than the genital will be singled out and this emotion directed elsewhere – to the feet, as among Chinese women of past generations, or to the face, as with Mohammedan women. Native Brazilian women are extremely unwilling to remove their nose plugs and Alaskan women to remove their enormous labrets. Feelings of shame may also be associated with types of behavior not connected with clothing. Perfectly naked savages, for example, show acute feelings of shame at seeing anyone eat in public.

All the other theories of the origin of clothing contain varied amounts of truth. The advocates have erred only in too generalized a support of their particular positions. It is not necessary to deny any of them, once one has granted that human custom has no unique root but in different parts of the world has been the result of quite different circumstances and habits of mind variously interacting.

Thus Frazer and Karsten argue for the origin of clothing in ideas of magic, as, for example, the covering of the organs of reproduction in order to prevent the evil eye being cast upon them. Amulets hung about the neck or inserted in the lip or the nose are the full scope of clothing among some peoples, and in those and similar cases costume can be most pertinently studied in connection with local magical beliefs. In some regions these have had a profound influence upon the development of dress, but it is not necessary to generalize them as the origin of clothing.

The theory that clothing originated in protection against the rigors of climate is defended by Knight Dunlap. To doubt that weather has ever been a factor would be to cast a gratuitous slur on human intelligence and to ignore one of the great differentiations between human and animal behavior. If it were the primary factor, however, the primitive tribes living in the cold climates of the southern hemisphere would have provided for themselves as well as those living in similar climates of the northern hemisphere. But they have not done so. For the freezing weather to which they are seasonally exposed the Australians and the Fuegians do not make themselves clothing but barely protect their shoulders with a skin. Certainly many other motivations have been as potent in the history of clothing as protection against the weather.

Westermarck considers dress under the heading of "Primitive Means of Attraction." He believes that it is fundamentally rooted in the erotic impulses. Instances of this sort have been given above and he presents many others, both of habitual ornamentation of the pubic coverings and of ornamentation worn for particular occasions, such as dances, especially those of a licentious character. The history of clothing in our own civilization is ample evidence of the degree to which one sex dresses for the other, and certainly the often recurring differentiation of the dresses of the two sexes should be studied from this angle.

It does not seem necessary, however, to single out the one trait of display before the opposite sex when dress is so obviously and so often a self-display on all counts. Sex display in dress may hardly appear in a given area, but display of trophies or display of status may be fundamental. Thus on the plains of North America men's dress is a heraldic display of war counts, and on the northwest coast a man's hat will be built up in cumulative units to designate his rank. As an old explorer said of the Fuegians, "although they are content to be naked, they are very ambitious to be fine." This impulse toward decoration is the most constantly recurring motivation in the history of clothing and, as we saw above, the one which is found also among the higher apes.

Modern conditions have introduced only one important factor into human behavior in regard to clothing. In all that has been said above, modern dress like that of any other period is merely one of many possible varieties all illustrative of the general principles. But there is one fundamental difference. Whereas in simpler conditions, even in untouched rural districts of Europe today, dress is geographically differentiated, in modern civilization it is temporally differentiated. This rise of fashion in the field of dress had begun somewhat tentatively between the tenth and the fourteenth century, but it is with the Renaissance that its full and startling effect is first to be gauged. In rural districts dress remained and has remained to the present time a matter of local individuality perpetuated for centuries with great conservatism. The revolutionary rise of fashion had to do only with the urban population and even more specifically with the court. Its onset in the fifteenth century was marked by those peculiarities that have continued to characterize fashion in the modern world: first, the grotesque exaggeration of certain features, in this case notably the hennin (the fantastically elongated head dress that was held on by a chin band); and second, the personal arbitership of the great lady, which is said to have been already a well developed role of Isabelle of Bavaria, wife of Charles VI.

From this period fashion has been of unceasing importance in the field of dress. The latter part of the fifteenth century and the earlier part of the sixteenth show some of the most pleasing of all western European fashions, styles that are best known through the portraits of the Italian Renaissance. In the first half of the sixteenth century the woman's hoop skirt was elaborated, and this returned in extreme forms in the mid-eighteenth and mid-nineteenth centuries, in less extreme form in the mid-seventeenth. In the eighteenth century version in the reign of Louis XVI this was coupled with spectacular display of costly material in garments; clothes became a primary means for the ostentatious exhibition of wealth. The greatest excesses were cultivated in the matter of hairdressing; coiffures were a half yard high and prints show the hairdressers seated on ladders in order to reach the upper tiers of their creations. Nor was there any marked improvement during the nineteenth century. Probably the fashions of the period from 1830 to 1900 – the desperately constricted waist, the bustle and the heavy dragging skirt – were the ugliest and most unhealthful in the history of women's dress in western civilization.

The usual view of fashion is, first, that it is an affair of violent contrasts, each few years' swing of the pendulum reversing that of the preceding; and second, that it is essentially dictated by individual Parisian costumers. Kroeber, however, taking as a test case woman's full dress toilette from 1844 to 1919, has shown that, at least in the measurements he has considered, fashion's vagaries follow definite long time trends. This is clearest in the measurement of the width of the skirt, which for fifty years before 1919 had in spite of incidental variations become progressively more constricted. For almost as long a period previously it had in the same way grown progressively fuller, and its cycle therefore would be about one hundred years. The length of the skirt showed a similar trend. Its cycle for this period was about a third the duration of the width cycle, but even this is too long to be due to the influence of a single gifted designer. Kroeber does not claim universal validity for his examples but draws from them two conclusions: first, in a broader view styles not merely oscillate between two points but work themselves out in cycles of considerable length; second, these cycles are obviously longer than the reign of influence of any one designer and are therefore independent even of the most powerful costumer.

The study of fashion along with a variety of other cultural traits of modern civilization, such as mass production, can derive no assistance from the history of the world before comparatively modern times. Fashion is new in human history and its future course is not known. At present it marks, as Santayana says, that margin of irresponsible variation in manners and thoughts which among a people artificially civilized may so easily be larger than the solid core. It may well be that this swift succession of styles will maintain itself as a fixed characteristic of dress as a culture trait in our civilization.

Source   Benedict, R. (1931). Dress. *Encyclopedia of the social sciences* (Vol. 5, 235–237). New York: Macmillan.

Biographical note   Ruth Fulton Benedict (1887–1948) was an American cultural anthropologist considered a pioneer in the study of how personality is shaped by culture. In fact, in her popular book *Patterns of Culture* (1934), she noted that a society's culture was "personality writ large" (p. vii). She studied with Franz Boas at Columbia and was one of the first women to earn a doctorate in anthropology, received in 1923 from Columbia University where she taught throughout her career. She focused her work on religious beliefs and practices, specifically studying American Plains Indians and Japanese culture.

References

Dunlap, K. (1928). The development and function of clothing. *Journal of General Psychology*, 1, 64–78.

Flügel, J. (1930). The psychology of clothes. London.

Frazer, J.G. (1910) *Totemism and exogamy*, 4 vols. London. Vol. iv, pp. 194, 200–2, 207.

Havelock, E. (1913). *The evolution of modesty, Studies in the psychology of sex.* (3rd ed.) Philadelphia.

Kroeber, A. (1919). On the principle of order in civilization as exemplified by changes in fashion. *American Anthropologist*, 21, 235–263.

Lowie, R. (1929). *Are we civilized?* New York.

Parsons, F. (1920). The psychology of dress. New York.

Westermarck, E.A.(1921). *The history of human marriage* (5th ed.). London.

Wissler, C. (1922). *The American Indian* (2nd ed.). New York.

* * *

Costume and Ideologies *Hilaire Hiler and Meyer Hiler*

Theories

Such considerations take us back to the very origins of clothing which are so closely connected with the generally fundamental psychology of the subject that they may appropriately be treated with it. For a more detailed discussion of these origins the reader is again referred to *From Nudity to Raiment*, Chapter V, and the references therein.[1] Here it may suffice to outline some of the more generally accepted theories referring, for purposes of further study, to the authors who respectively support them.

The Theory of Sex Attraction, based to some extent on Montaigne's statement that "There are certain things which are hidden in order to be shown" is best explained in brief by Westermarck, in his *History of Human Marriage*, where he declares that "we have every reason to believe that mere decorations have also developed into clothes" and that clothing originated mainly "in the desire of men and women to make themselves mutually attractive." This theory is supported by Havelock Ellis (with reservations), Grosse and others.

That it is in direct opposition to the Mosaic Theory as expounded in the Bible, and the Theory of Possession held by Ratzel and other early ethnologists, both the author and the authorities quoted above, are well aware.

The Taboo Theory, self-explanatory in its title, was put forward by Durkheim and supported by Reinach. The latter says that "Durkheim determined it happily in recognizing the *blood taboo* as a particular case." It would seem reasonable to suppose that Freud would be interested in this theory and with the possible exception to be mentioned later, lend it his support.

The Totemistic Theory, as advanced by Crawley in his *Mystic Rose*, argues for an amuletic origin, claiming that ornamentation, tattooing, etc., may have originated "for the purpose of magically insulating certain organs." We are unacquainted with any important defense or elaboration of this theory on the part of others.

The Amuletic Theory, is closely related to Crawley's, as may be also the idea that clothing originated in the carrying of trophies or trophyistic surrogates.

I advanced an Esthetic Theory based upon substantiated observations of the behavior of birds and animals with arboreally developed vision, such as bower birds, jackdaws, monkeys and apes. Attraction for shiny objects may have suggested that they might most easily be kept near the possessor by being attached to the person. Köhler, in *The Mentality of Apes*; Edmond Haraucourt, in *Daah, le Premier Homme*; and Johannes V. Jensen in *The Long Journey* directly or indirectly seem to support this theory.

It now seems that an interesting if somewhat complex theory might also be built up on the Castration Fear so important in Freudian Psycho-analysis. Quite apart from any directly protective function of the garment, this fear may well be the basis for the amuletic theory. If men, as their more elaborate

1. Hiler, H. (1929). *From nudity to raiment*. London: W. and G. Foyle.

dress in primitive stages of society may indicate, wore ornament or clothing before women did, a Castration Theory becomes more plausible.

We can think of a few other factors which come into the psychology of clothing with an advancingly complex social structure. They touch upon economic factors increasingly as these in their turn interact with others. Certain objects and substances which may have owed their first importance to esthetic and amuletic considerations take on an economic value and tend to function as a primitive media of exchange. Wampum, shells, teeth, skins, etc., and finally leather and metals.

Caste and heraldry as manifested by dress seem to have an economic basis discernable at some early stage. Hunting was certainly an economic activity and the prowess of the hunter must have automatically been made evident. Prestige and prestige-imitation, still a powerful conditioner of dress, appear, flourish and evolve in diversified and ever elaborate forms.

Source Excerpted from Hiler, H., & Hiler, M. (1939). *Bibliography of costume*. New York: H.W. Wilson Company.

Biographical note Hilaire Hiler (1898-1966) was an American artist working in the expressionist style. He worked for the WPA as a muralist and print-maker. His first book, *From Nudity to Raiment: An Introduction to the Study of Costume History*, was published in 1929. The research for that book evolved into one of the most comprehensive bibliographies of the period, co-edited with his father, Meyer Hiler.

2

Physical Connections between the Body and Dress

The Psychology of Clothing George Van Ness Dearborn

The science of clothing so far has never been developed; it is something new, almost pioneer scientific work. The personal science of clothes and of being clothed, then, is the topic on which I would suggest a few considerations from a somewhat technical point of view.

It includes, as I shall consider it, two phases, first, a physiological psychology of clothing, and then the beginnings of the applied psychology of clothing. These complement each other. All this is a new application of psychology (the general science of how to live), and one of which the great public is much in real need. The public, to be sure, does not realize this need, any more than it knew that it was in pressing need of information on diet or on sex or on other things. The public does need basic scientific information on how to clothe themselves properly so that they will be both more efficient and more happy, because continually more comfortable.

I. *The Satisfaction-Efficiency Ratio* – Underlying this whole matter of the physiology and the psychology of clothing is an ancient idea which is of fundamental importance throughout the whole matter. In the lectures to my students I give it the technical name of the then-euphoric index or ratio – but we wont worry about the name. Sthen and euphor are two Greek terms; sthen stands for strength or energy, and euphor for well-bearing, contentment, well-being, happiness; while ratio, of course, or "index," is the relationship between the other two. The old and simple enough idea then, is, to put it wholly outside of scientific terms, that one expends more energy and is therefore more efficient in many ways when he is contented and happy, using the word happy as a symbol for the broad translation of the general Greek term euphoria. When a person is satisfied, contented, in good humor, when he is "happy," in short, he expends more energy, has more initiative, and is altogether more efficient than when he is unhappy, worrying about something, or when he "has a grouch," or any other of the conditions opposite to happiness. *Freedom from discomfort* underlies it. It importantly underlies the psychology of clothing in particular, without any doubt at all, because personal comfort is absolutely essential "in the long run" to a high-grade of efficiency in the long life-run. This is not so much true of an Eastport man for example feeding sheets of tin to a sardine-box stamping machine, but it is true of any kind of work which involves the optimum action of the "higher" and freer phases of the mind and skilled body. Comfort in general is indispensable to ideal behaviour that is at all free.

Comfort has both a physiological and a psychological aspect; but both aspects underlie efficiency in a way which is measurable even in dollars and cents. The factory-managers, as you already are aware, not many years ago started out to prompt their employees and operatives to maintain better health, to keep them in better "condition;" finding that it was a "good policy," even as income was concerned, to go so far as to hire a "doctor" at two or three thousand a year to help keep the employees well.

. . . The present discussion concerns first the physiological psychology of clothes. My approach in this knowledge is mostly that of pure science from the universities and from the psychological and physiological laboratories, although no actual researches that I am able to hear of have as yet been done in a scientific laboratory on the psychology of clothing . . .

. . . There is much more physiology in the science of adequate clothing as a process than most men, even the physiologists, would at first suspect. And yet it is obvious, on thought for a moment, that any covering as heavy, as complete, and as relatively rigid as an average suit of clothes or a proper gown could not help having multiform influences within and without over the body which wears it. Because so universal and so continuous, these influences are of noteworthy scientific and practical importance.

The reason in a nutshell for this is that one's clothes are one of the important things that intervenes between the individual personality and his environment, and you understand that life itself in a sense is a reaction of an individual to his environment. As Webb puts it, "As a matter of fact, our artificial coverings have become so much a part of our life that one may perhaps be allowed to apply the methods of the naturalist to their consideration, and deal with them as if they were part and parcel of the creature which wears them" – as pragmatically they are. We might almost consider clothes as a vicarious or artificial skin, almost an extension of the individual's boundary, involving important relationships between the person and his environment, spiritual as much as material. And that is the reason, the deeply fundamental reason, why there is so much real science in the physiology and the psychology of clothing, subjective and objective, personally and socially and industrially.

Let us take up first then the discussion of the physiological psychology of clothes in three groups of relations: 1. to the skin; 2. to bodily action or behavior; and 3. to body-temperature. Since the centuries – those slow, groping, aspiring centuries – when manhood and womanhood were new and our preprogenitors were covered with a fairly thick mantle of hair, the human animal man has been a naturally *naked* creature. He naturally is so, still. For a reason none too easily apprehended, there seems to us something ludicrous in this nakedness of the nâive savage. Thomas Hood the Younger, for example, almost blushes as he tells us

> "And their principle clothes were a ring through the nose
> And a patch of red paint on the forehead,"

while other poetasters less known to fame than Thomas Hood, and escaped missionaries and cartoonists innumerable have almost vied with each other in expressing in memorable phrases the insistent natural nakedness, always adorned, of natural man. This interesting and important negative phase of our subject we must for the present all but ignore.

The human animal is naturally, if you please, then, and normally a naked animal, and up to within about three hundred years ago people were allowed to live in corners of Europe, specially in Ireland and in Germany (Rudeck), naked. Up to three centuries ago, at least, the nakedness of the primeval man had not become so entirely "immodest" that it was prohibited by enforced law. Man is naturally a naked animal, and it takes a very long time indeed to adapt an organism to artificial, "acquired" new conditions. Furless and with little hair was primeval man; and he still likes to be so.

In clothing him, therefore, one has to respect and not ignore this natural nakedness; and especially the basal fact that man gets his highest comfort when naturally warm environmental air is freely playing over and on his skin. You all know, of course, the delight of exposure to the breeze, and to warm showers, and to other conditions of the natural environment, when you are naked.

Now, this basic principle of the physiology of clothes, (that man is constructed for efficiency-with-happiness, primally as a *naked* animal) requires that he be rather careful in adapting ideal clothing to his requirements, because man, after all, is a highly sensitive being. His efficiency is an intricate and a rather susceptible thing, and has to be catered to, if he is to get the most out of his few and flying years.

Source Excerpted from Dearborn, G. (1918). The psychology of clothing. *The Psychological Monographs, 26,* 1–72.

Biographical note George Van Ness Dearborn (1898–1938) was a physician practicing in the United States.

Reference

Webb, W.M. (1907). *The heritage of dress*. London: E.G. Richards.

* * *

Microcosmus: An Essay Concerning Man and His Relation to the World *Hermann Lotze*

. . . Not only, however, with this aesthetic enjoyment do we sympathetically expand our sentience beyond the limits of our body, but also, when we desire with practical aims to modify the outer world, we are aided in the calculation of its relations by a similar projection outwards of our imagination, put within our power by the delicacy of our sense of touch and the ease with which we combine past experience. The skin surface of our body is not at all points so organized that it can, by the production of different local signs, discriminate the stimulations of their immediately contiguous points, and call up in consciousness different sensations answering to them, and consequently an image of their combination, form, and situation . . .

Of all living beings, man is the only one that from his natural defenceless-ness is forced to use implements in order to attain his ends. The capacity for using them depends not only on the muscular power or the arm, but to a very large extent on delicacy of sensation and an extraordinary ease and certainty in associating ideas. If a rod lightly grasped is lying in our hand, so that its motions have some free play, it presses the surface of our skin at various points. The apparently direct feeling which we have at every moment of the position of our limbs, teaches us to judge whether these momentarily pressed spots of our hand can be connected together by a straight or a curved, a vertical or a horizontal line; we ascribe the same form and position to the rod that causes these sensations . . .

. . . Not only the hands but the whole body is capable of similar perceptions, though with different degrees of delicacy in different parts, and often with the assistance of other conditions. The unyielding stone below our feet causes a different feeling from the wooden step of a staircase or the rung of a ladder, both of which are by our weight set vibrating with various degrees of amplitude and velocity . . . These striking phenomena must be taken account of by those to whom the feeling which we are never without, of the outline, the position, and the movements of our own body seems explicable only on the supposition that the sentient soul is diffused or extended through the

Figure 2.1 "If a rod lightly grasped is lying in our hand . . ." Lotze calls objects of dress such as shoes, hats, and hand-held walking sticks "foreign bodies" in relationship with the surface of a human's body. He contends that they can extend not only a person's consciousness of their body but expand the self and the personality in such a way as to create strength, vigor, steadiness, or even a sense of power of being. From *The Delineator*, September 1907, New York: The Buttrick Publishing Co.

whole of the body. In the cases referred to the soul extends still farther; exactly the same persuasive illusion that made us before say it was in the finger-tips, makes us now say it is present – percipient and sentient – at the end of the stick, of the probe, of the needle . . .

. . . We speak of dress, to which we alone are impelled by an original instinct, that of the ape being merely one of imitation. We speak not of other points of view, which either do not deserve to be examined or must stand over to other opportunities, of the use of clothes as a protection against the inclemency of weather, of the sense of modesty that chooses them as a covering; our inquiry is exclusively as to the source of the pleasure, which they and other kinds of decoration afford to the human soul. It lies by no means only in the gratification of the vanity that seeks to be admired by others, but in the heightened and ennobled vital feeling of the wearer himself. The colours and the metallic lustre of the finery alone minister to the craving for outside admiration; in other respects our pleasure in ornament and dress is derived from the sensations which both excite in ourselves . . .

. . . Wherever, in fact, we bring a foreign body into relationship with the surface of our body – for it is not in the hand alone that these peculiarities are developed – the consciousness of our personal existence is prolonged into the extremities and surfaces of this foreign body, and the consequence is feelings now of an expansion of our proper self, now of the acquisition of a kind and amount of motion foreign to our natural organs, now of an unusual degree of vigour, power of resistance, or steadiness in our bearing.

The earliest stages of these feelings, to mention a few examples, is brought about by coverings for the head and feet, both peculiarly adapted to add something, at least apparently, to our height. Every form of head-gear represents in the perpendicular that passes through its centre of gravity the above-mentioned rod; its value for feeling is enhanced with its height and partly with its form, namely, when the result of the latter is a distribution of bulk such as perceptibly moves the centre of gravity upwards, and at the same time, in the swerve from the vertical direction, brings about a strong inclination towards one side that must be counteracted by a balancing effort of the muscles. The head-gear is of no use till there is a threatening of this want of balance: in equilibrium it is only a definite amount of weight; hence one intentionally puts on one's hat somewhat aslant, in order that one may always be aware of the distance between its highest inclined point and its plane of support, the head. Thus arises the pleasing delusion that we ourselves, our own life, and our strength reach up to that point, and at every step that shakes it, at every puff of wind that sets it in motion, we have quite distinctly the feeling as if a part of our own being were solemnly nodding backwards and forwards. Evidently, therefore, one feels quite differently in a cylindrical hat that encourages these emotions from what one does in a cap, the raised peak of which would perform the same office very imperfectly; and we come quite to understand the disposition (showing itself early and in low stages of culture, and perfected afterwards in higher ones), by means of high erect helmets, bearskin caps, and lofty coiffures, to fortify the consciousness of the wearer with the feeling of a majestic upward extension of his personality, as well as to increase the fear-inspiring or respect-inspiring effect of the figure on others . . .

The second class of these feelings we derive from all hanging and waving drapery, which, after the model of the ball set in revolving motion, agitates the surface of our body by a charming variety of extensions in different directions, and causes us to feel as if we were ourselves present in the gyrations of the freely-floating ends . . . The last form of those to which we referred is that assumed by our feelings under the influence of clothes in the strict sense. The greater or less tension and firmness possessed by the material in itself, or due to its cut, is transferred to us as if it resulted from our bearing. A corset resembles the above-mentioned hollow vessel, only that it is filled by the body, not at one point merely, but throughout its whole extent; on every occasion of contact with this stiff case the tension and firmness of its framework is felt exactly as if both properties belonged to our body; unquestionably this also is a means of imparting the feeling of a more vigorous and elastic existence . . .

Source Excerpted from Lotze, R.H. (1887). *Microcosmos: An essay concerning man and his relation to the world.* Edinburgh: T.T. Clark.

Biographical note Rudolf Hermann Lotze (1817–1881) was a German philosopher who was a student of both medicine and philosophy. He believed in the universality of scientific law and insisted that philosophy could be considered a natural science because both humans and inanimate objects were subject to natural laws. He held that knowledge was the result of observation and experimentation. This reading is drawn from Lotze's principle work on the theory of knowledge and reality.

Some Aspects of the Early Sense of Self *G. Stanley Hall*

II. Within the surface, the child's somatic consciousness does not at first penetrate. The skin is often pinched, pulled, scratched and otherwise explored; but is never thought of as a continuous limiting surface, at first, but later such questions as, "Could I jump out of it and another get in?" "Would it fit, stretch, shrink?" etc. "How could I get out of it?" "How would I look?" etc., are common. Much washing and rubbing develop the dermal consciousness and in several returns even itching and scratching provoke special attention to the skin. Children often take much satisfaction in stroking and "pooring" themselves and other persons, and if nervous acquire extreme sensitiveness to any degree of roughness. The most marked dermal impressions throughout childhood are thermal.

At the age of from 3 to 5 the bones are generally noticed, and there are many questions concerning the hard things under the skin. Some think them wood, iron, stone, etc. On learning that they are bone there are many flitting fears, sometimes that they will break or that dogs or other animals who love bones will eat them, or again that they have a horrid skeleton inside them, and there are many curious forms of weird bone fancies and scores of questions as to their purpose, material, size and shape. Often the knee-pan is the first bone in our returns to become an object of special interest; next comes the elbow, and then the wrist and joints. Bones are generally the first and for a time the chief object of curiosity within the body, and the discovery that cats and dogs have bones is often an event, and their size is often vastly magnified, and their shape curiously discussed.

Next comes the stomach. Its sensations of plethora and often pain, its associations with food and drink, are early. Many children believe that the entire internal body save the bones is a receptacle for food, and that it fills arms and legs, so that if the skin were anywhere cut, food would be found to be the stuffing. Some believe it hardens directly into bone. Often whims concerning appetite have affiliations with the weirdest kind of ideas of the alimentary tract. Many children conceive of the body as stuffed with saw-dust or with cotton like a pin-cushion, or with dust of which man was made, or else sweepings. On pricking or injuring the skin and seeing blood, many form the idea, often no doubt from inadequate answers to their questions, that the entire body is a skin or bag filled with blood and if it is tapped blood will gush out and the body collapse like a balloon. They often notice the pulsations of the heart and think some one is pounding inside them, and may even develop a definite image of how the man looks and how he strikes. Few organs inside the body excite so much curiosity as the heart, but the questions show that this is in large part due to its association with life and the soul, which is often identified with it even in form. Upon noticing the activity of respiration children almost always begin to experiment; they exhale all the residual breath possible and inhale a maximal amount, breathe as fast as possible and as slow, experiment with costal and abdominal modes, and particularly hold the breath often in rivalry with each other, the higher centres thus learning control of the reflex apparatus. Very many, too, are the questions – "Why do we breathe?" "Do animals, plants, God, etc., breathe?" "What is breath?" There are many morbid fears lest respiration should accidentally stop, and many children resolve to lie awake to prevent this calamity. At this time the claustraphobias may take their rise, and there develops unusual dread of being hugged, choked, smothered in close places, being shut into closets, trunks, etc. Some have for a long time the conception that the body is a bag of wind, and some children are panic stricken on seeing their breath on a frosty morning, thinking the soul is escaping. Perhaps there was some truth in the antique conception that dreams objectified this function, and when in nightmare we seem to flutter and hover, it is the lungs which play the stimulating rôle and suggest the thought of wings.

It is a revelation of great significance if this inward direction of thought has been aroused to learn what the country boy finds out on butchering day. Such experiences, although slight and without demonstration, cause a great and wholesome readjustment of this aspect of self-consciousness by showing both the nature and the relation of the parts within. The two most frequent questions throughout are, first, "Why have I stomach, eyes, hands?" etc., or a question seeking purpose and use; and secondly; "Have other human beings or animals the same organs?" And to realize that parents, playmates, or dog, horse and cow have legs, eyes, teeth, ears, stomach and heart as they have, always excites interest and pleasure. No child, of course, has all these experiences in the foreground of its consciousness, but all have some, and doubtless pass through, some more and some less consciously, all these phases, the definite order of most of which still remains to be determined. The internal sensations and conceptions are, as we shall see later, those most intimately associated with childish conceptions of the soul.

III. The third element in the child's consciousness, but not usually included as a factor of the ego, but which must not be neglected, and on which our returns are voluminous, is dress and adornment. Rings for fingers or ears, shoes and gloves attract the child's attention to the part involved, and a change of dress often involves change of disposition, and almost character. During the second year this is often strongly developed. Corresponding perhaps to the prominent position of the foot in the infantile consciousness, a new pair of shoes seems quite as important as a new dress. Far later, too, gloves come into great prominence. Very striking with young children is the charm of some single and perhaps small feature, as, e.g., a pair of shoes with buckles, stockings with clocks, jacket with bright buttons, a hat with a feather, a bit of fur here or ribbon there, a sash with buckle. So, too, the first pocket, the first trousers, suspenders, long pants or dress, first watch, parasol, muff, gloves, ring, necklace, standing collar, perfumery, new ways of wearing the hair, the first belt, breastpin, veil – all these stand out in memory in the most vivid way, and have played an important rôle in the education of self-consciousness. The passion to have new things noticed, which often makes children so ridiculous, seems sometimes strongest to strangers and sometimes towards friends. This seems to mark an important moral distinction. For most girls all new articles of dress and ornament become doubly dear if liked or admired by those they know and love best, and lose their charm if the latter do not care for them.

Lotze rather curiously thought he had done for personal adornment a service comparable to what Kepler had done for astronomy by his three laws, in which he believed he had explained man's satisfaction in dress. If we touch an object with a stick, we instinctively analyze our sensations into those felt by contact of the hand with the stick, and ascribe the rest to the object at the other end of it. It gives us thus a peculiar pleasure when consciousness runs through all that touches us, and this we feel in those articles of attire that lengthen the body by prolongations of our personality at the head or feet – high shoes, stilts, hats, head-dress etc. He thinks that all these forms of feeling change with every change of their height and form, which shifts the centre of gravity, and there is special satisfaction when equilibrium is the least trifle in danger. We feel the wind or our own motions by very different sensations in hats that are high, broad, obliquely placed, or heavy. Secondly, all hanging, fluttering or swinging garments, by their change of tension in different directions, cause us to feel ourselves most agreeably in the peripheral tract or graceful curves of their free moving ends: a trail dragging along the earth is like a new organ, endowing us with a new sense. Rings, ribbons, ear-rings, watches, sashes and everything that hangs and dangles are worn especially by the young, not so much for display as to gratify the exquisite pressure sense so peculiar to them and which, according to the modern fashions, free, flowing hair no longer does. Lastly the impressions we derive from our own clothing and its strength, stiffness or thickness our self-feeling imputes to the form or poise of our own body. The pressure of a corset, Lotze thinks, awakens the feeling of a stronger and more elastic existence; so girdles, bracelets, and above all the first pair of trousers with suspenders gives a pleasing sense of sturdy inflexibility, and uprightness. If this view is correct it follows that we admire the folds of a graceful, well-fitting garment, not for its beauty, but that we unconsciously reproduce in ourselves the agreeable sensation of the wearer's body. So the false arm or leg half deceives even the wearer as to the boundaries of his own corporeal existence.

This view is very extreme. The great pleasure in wearing new and beautiful objects of attire in childhood is to secure thereby the attention and interest of others. Our returns abound in accounts of children who display and pro-trude new articles of dress, or call attention to them in the most vain and laughable way. Moreover the fact that even children will wear thin clothes when heavy ones would be far more comfortable, shoes that are too small for the sake of looks, and garments that are uncomfortably tight or thin in places, shows the dominance of those functions which Lotze disregards. The chief question is, and especially with girls, not how attire feels, but how it looks, and this standpoint dominates often in those garments that are not seen. The child who is habitually well dressed learns to avoid acts and environments which tend to soil his clothes and may become dainty, finical, fastidious and effeminate. The child who is rudely and poorly dressed, on the other hand, comes in closer contact with the world about him and acquires a knowledge more real and substantial. It is difficult to determine which pleasure is the greater, that of habitually well dressed children when very exceptionally allowed to put on old garments that cannot be injured and to strip head and feet and abandon themselves to the natural freedom thus given, or of very poorly clad children who by some good fortune are provided with attire that enables them to feel the great luxury of being well dressed. Children sometimes develop an insistent impulse to strip off parts of and occasionally all of their clothing, partly from sheer discomfort. Pants as usually made are an unphysiological and unhygienic garment, and much might be said in favor of a more rational dress for hips and thighs. There are cases of persistent denudations in childhood that are morbid and atavistic. Of the three functions of clothes, protection, ornament and Lotzean self-feeling, we must, I think, conclude that while the first is more important, the last is most infrequent and the second by far the most conspicuous in childhood. Many mention a corroding kind of self-pity with which they regard an old garment after it has been superseded by a newer and better one, and others preserve for themselves and later for their children all the articles of the dress of childhood and infancy, and regard them later with feelings curiously described, and no doubt still more curiously mingled. That, however, man's primitive body consciousness has been largely disguised and translated into clothes-consciousness, there can be no doubt. The comfort of clean garments, sensitiveness to texture and thickness, flexibility and fit are elements which are no doubt always present, and Lotze has done a real service in showing us that clothes are an integral part of our self-consciousness. The love of wearing the dress of adults may be interpreted thus, but clothes are at best alter ego and also in part mask and distort the primal sense of the physical self. Cleanliness of body like clean dress has a prodigious moral effect on children, who change manners, temper, conduct, and put on a better self after being well washed. A wise application of clothes-psychology can do very much in rightly poising a child at the golden mean between too much and too little self-consciousness if not between excessive shyness and over-boldness.

. . . A person is a vast aggregate of qualities and influences vinculated together, treated and acting as a unit. After Cicero many ancient and medieval works on oratory listed the traits of an ideal socius, best calculated to influence men, and most worthy of respect, or most provocative of imitation. First was form, figure, complexion, and the factors of physical beauty, fine eyes, nose, chin, bust, foot, hand, shoulders, etc., the contour of any one of which might have a perfection that was ravishing, and if truly put in marble would make a sculptor immortal. Physical beauty is an immense power, and ugliness is an eternal disadvantage. Next come dress and toilet, with every detail of hair, nails, shoes, head-gear, proper fashions, and even cosmetics, perfumery, etc., if and where needed, correct taste which is the beginning of art and which remedies defects of form, all of which are subjects worthy of long and detailed study as sources of proper personal influence. Third come the automatisms, which are among the most important media of likes and dislikes, and even fetishisms, tricks of articulation, of facial expression, bearing and carriage, the use of the voice, positions and movements of hands and feet, smiling and laughing, habits of fan, handkerchief, napkin, knife and fork, gesture, inflection, all the minor morals of manners, the magnetic aura, atmosphere, presence, style, which reflect all one's environment, breeding and heredity, and which because they are unconscious reveal the true self that words, social forms and conventionalities so often hide. Then come the voluntary actions, either deeds accomplished or abilities which mark the range of the ego of will. What can one do? How would he act under the strain of jealousy, anger, love, fear, temptation, and in any possible condition? What is the vocational sphere of action? Where would character give way? Self-control be lost? And how much energy is there? Fifth, what are the quality and flux of the habitual currents of feeling? The temperament and dominant sentiments? Is there the hearty euphoria of that good fellowship which covers a multitude of sins the good heart that is Prince Hal's "sun and moon?" Does duty rule? Or is the soul weakened by self-indulgence? Is it malevolent? Tricky? Hypercritical? How will it stand the strain of disappointment or affection? Of publicity? Of fame? Of fatigue? Is it stable or moody? Harmonious or unbalanced? Sickly? Self-conscious and morbid? or Hearty? Eupeptic? or Eucholic? Then, and far less prominent than we think, come the mental equipment or intellectual possessions of culture, the size of the fund of knowledge, the inventory of mental resources, and especially the breadth and height of sympathies, both for persons and ideas, the range of interests, the judgment and sense in the use of knowledge, originality, and independence of thought. If to these we add the still more adventitious advantages of fame, wealth, birth and name, we shall have a magazine of influences which has a power to hold other souls up together and to keep them occupied and well directed, the vast and manifold beneficence of which psychology is still unable to trace . . .

Source   Excerpted from Hall, G.S. (1898). Some aspects of the early sense of self. *American Journal of Psychology*, 351–395.

Biographical note   Granville Stanley Hall (1844–1924) was a pioneer in establishing psychology in the U.S. He earned, at Harvard, the first doctorate in psychology awarded in the U.S. He set up the first formal psychology laboratory in the U.S., at Johns Hopkins University. A founder of developmental psychology, Hall claimed that humans pass through the same developmental stages as non-humans. He founded several publications and was a founder and first president of the American Psychological Association.

3

Health Issues and Dress Reform

Fashion in Deformity *William Henry Flower*

The propensity to *deform*, or alter from the natural form, some part of the body, is one which is common to human nature in every aspect in which we are acquainted with it, the most primitive and barbarous, and the most civilized and refined.

The alterations or deformities which it is proposed to consider in this essay, are those which are performed, not by isolated individuals, or with definite motives, but by considerable numbers of members of a community, simply in imitation of one another – in fact, according to *fashion* "that most inexorable tyrant to which the greater part of mankind are willing slaves."

Fashion is now often associated with change, but in less civilized conditions of society fashions of all sorts are more permanent than with us; and in all communities such fashions as those here treated of are, for obvious reasons, far less likely to be subject to the fluctuations of caprice than those affecting the dress only, which, even in Shakespeare's time, changed so often that "the fashion wears out more apparel than the man." Alterations once made in the form of the body cannot be discarded or modified in the lifetime of the individual, and therefore, as fashion is intrinsically imitative, such alterations have the strongest possible tendency to be reproduced generation after generation.

The origins of these fashions are mostly lost in obscurity, all attempts to solve them being little more than guesses. Some of them have become associated with religious or superstitious observances, and so have been spread and perpetuated; some have been vaguely thought to be hygienic in motive; most have some relation to conventional standards of improved personal appearance; but whatever their origin, the desire to conform to common usage, and not to appear singular, is the prevailing motive which leads to their continuance. They are perpetuated by imitation, which, as Herbert Spencer says, may result from two widely divergent motives. It may be prompted by reverence for one imitated, or it may be prompted by the desire to assert equality with him . . .

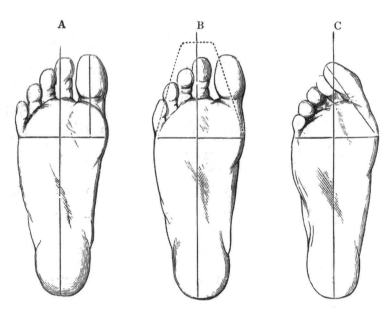

FIG. 17.—A. Natural form of the sole of the Foot, the great toe parallel to the axis of the whole foot. B. The same, with outline of ordinary fashionable boot. C. The modification of the form of the foot, necessarily produced by wearing such a boot.

Figure 3.1 ". . . everything which is beautiful and excellent in the human foot destroyed . . ." Flower compared European footwear to Chinese foot binding as "only a slight step in excess." He used these three illustrations to display graphically the serious foot deformities caused by fashionable European boots. Three forms of the foot – a) natural, b) with fashionable boot shape, c) boot deformity from *Fashion in Deformity* (p. 64), W.H. Flower, 1881, London: Macmillan and Co.

    The feet have suffered more, and altogether with more serious results to general health and comfort, from simple conformity to pernicious customs, than any other part of the body. And on this subject, instead of relating the unaccountable caprices of the savage, we have to speak only of people who have already advanced to a tolerably high grade of civilization, and to include all those who are at the present time foremost in the ranks of intellectual culture.

    The most extreme instance of modification of the size and form of the foot in obedience to fashion, is the well-known case of the Chinese women, not entirely confined to the highest classes, but in some districts pervading all grades of society alike. The deformity is produced by applying tight band-ages round the feet of the girls when about five years old. The bandages are specially manufactured, Miss Norwood[1] tells us, and are about two inches wide and two yards long for the first year, five yards long for subsequent years. The end of the strip is laid on the inside of the foot at the instep, then carried over the toes, under the foot and round the heel, the toes being thus drawn towards and across the sole, while a bulge is produced in the instep and a deep indentation in the sole. Successive layers of bandage are wound round the foot until the strip is all used, and the end is then sewn tightly down. After a month the foot is put in hot water to soak some time; then the bandage is carefully unwound. Notwithstanding the powdered alum and other of the sole. The whole has now the appearance of the hoof of some animal rather than a human foot, and affords a very inefficient organ of support, as the peculiar tottering gait of those possessing it clearly shows. When once formed, the "golden lily," as the Chinese lady calls her delicate little foot, can never recover its original shape.

But strange as this custom seems to us, it is only a slight step in excess of what the majority of people in Europe subject themselves and their children to. From personal observation of a large number of feet of persons of all ages and of all classes of society in our own country, I do not hesitate to say that there are very few, if any, to be met with that do not, in some degree, bear evidence of having been subjected to a compressing influence more or less injurious. Let any one take the trouble to inquire into what a foot ought to be. For external form look at any of the antique models – the nude Hercules Farnese or the sandaled Apollo Belvidere; watch the beautiful freedom of motion in the wide spreading toes of an infant; consider the wonderful mechanical contrivances for combining strength with mobility, firmness with flexibility; the numerous bones, articulations, ligaments; the great toe, with seven special muscles to give it that versatility of motion which was intended that it should possess – and then see what a miserable, stiffened, distorted thing is this same foot, when it has been submitted for a number of years to the "improving" process to which our civilization condemns it. The toes all squeezed and flattened against each other; the great toe no longer in its normal position, but turned outwards, pressing so upon the others that one or more of them frequently has to find room for itself either above or under its fellows; the joints all rigid, the muscles atrophied and powerless; the finely formed arch broken down; everything which is beautiful and excellent in the human foot destroyed – to say nothing of the more serious evils which so generally follow – corns, bunions, in-growing nails, and all their attendant miseries.

---

1. American missionary at Swatow, *Times*, Sept. 2, 1880.

It is not only leathern boots and shoes that are to blame for producing alterations in the form of the feet; even the stocking, comparatively soft and pliable as it is, when made with pointed toes and similar form for both sides, must take its share. The continual, steady, though gentle pressure, keeps the toes squeezed together, and especially hinders the recovery of its proper form and mobility, when attempts at curing a misshapen foot are being made by wearing shoes of rational construction. Socks adapted to the different form of the two feet, or "rights and lefts," are occasionally to be met with at hosiers, and it would add greatly to comfort if they were more generally adopted. For some cases it is well to have them made with distinct toes like gloves. With such socks and properly constructed shoes, a much distorted foot, even of a middle aged person, will raising and propelling the body. Turning out the toes is, moreover, a common cause of weak ankles, as it throws the weight of the body chiefly on the inside, instead of distributing it equally over all parts of the joint . . .

The fact is, that in admiring such distorted forms as the . . . symmetrically pointed foot, we are opposing our judgment to that of the Maker of our bodies; we are neglecting the criterion afforded by nature; we are departing from the highest standard of classical antiquity; we are simply putting ourselves on a level in point of taste with those Australians, Botocudos, and Negroes. We are taking fashion, and nothing better, higher, or truer, for our guide; and after the various examples which have now been brought forward, may we not well ask, with Shakespeare,

"SEEST THOU NOT, WHAT A DEFORMED THIEF THIS FASHION IS?"

Source   Excerpted from Flower, W.H. (1881). *Fashion in deformity*. London: MacMillan.

Biographical note   Sir William Henry Flower (1831–1899) was a medical doctor, a surgeon, and professor of comparative anatomy. The reading comes from an essay that was delivered as a lecture to the Royal Institution of Great Britain and subsequently published in their proceedings.

❖ ❖ ❖

The Science of Dress *Ada S. Ballin*

. . . The chief evil, however, of ordinary dress, results from the way in which it is supported, pressing upon the waist, hindering the development of the internal organs and cramping them, thus tending to produce injuries which may affect the happiness of the girl's future.

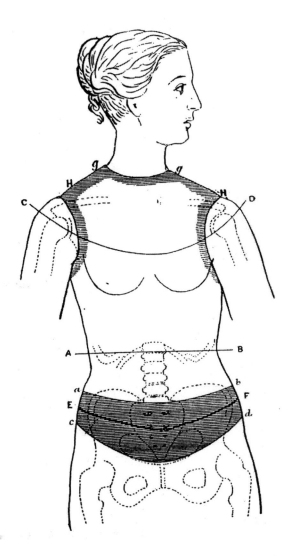

Figure 3.2 Ballin used this illustration in her book to describe how the weight of
clothing could potentially cause damage and injuries to a woman's
body. Line C–D shows how the lowered neckline of a chemise or
low-set sleeves drag down on the shoulders, preventing a woman
from raising her arms over her head and eventually causing rounded,
forward-sloping shoulders. Line A–B shows how the weight of a skirt
and bodice hangs incorrectly from the waist, pressing in on the pelvis.
Lines E–F and G–H are the best areas to properly support garments.
Plate 5 from *The Science of Dress in Theory and Practice* (across from
p. 174), by A.S. Ballin, 1885, London: Sampson, Low, Marston, Searle,
and Rivington.

I believe that a large number of the cases of curvature of the spine met with in surgical practice, generally in girls between the ages of twelve and sixteen, result directly or indirectly from the weight and improper pressure of clothes, a potent agent in causing the deformity being the wearing of high-heeled boots, which throw the body forward in walking. Tight, stiff stays are responsible for a great deal of harm, and I am afraid that horrible process called tight-lacing begins but too frequently earlier than is generally suspected.

I propose to deal with these evils seriatim, and show how best they may be avoided.

I have already given what seem to me sufficient reasons for maintaining that wool is the natural and most healthy substance out of which to manufacture clothes. Clothes in their action should be merely supplementary to the skin, and care is required to enable them to properly perform the functions demanded of them. They should be light, warm, permit free transpiration, or, in other words, ventilate well; they should exert no pressure on any part, and they should be free from all poisonous particles, whether of dirt or of dye.

Our bodies lose heat by evaporation, and also by conduction, convection, and radiation. We, therefore, require our clothes to be absorbent, so that the evaporation shall not take place on the skin, but from the surface of the clothes, which prevents chill. The mere fact of covering impedes loss of heat by convection, and radiation, and provided our garments are made of non-conducting materials they necessarily minimize that loss of heat by conduction which is always going on between two bodies of different temperatures, such as the human body and the air, just on the same principle that a tea-cosy retains heat in the teapot. We stuff our tea-cosies with wool in perhaps unconscious obedience to the principles I have explained, and we should clothe our bodies in the same way.

Stationary air, as has been observed, is a bad conductor of heat; but particles of air rise, when heated, and give place to colder ones. Hence it is desirable that the covering of the body should have a rough surface, so as to entangle in it particles of air, which becoming heated, and being unable to rise, form a sort of warm atmosphere round the body. It is an advantage, moreover, for garments to be loosely woven, so that a certain quantity of air may be entangled in the meshes of the material, and for the same reason, instead of the clothes consisting of one very thick garment, successive layers of clothing are and should be worn, as a considerable amount of air is then imprisoned between them.

The human body has a tiny atmosphere clinging to its hairs, in proportion to their size, as may be seen by plunging the hand quickly into water, and then holding it still, when little silvery bubbles will be seen on the skin. But in other animals better covered than man, air adheres in considerable quantities to the thick hair, fur, wool, and feathers, adding to their warmth-saving capabilities, and here again wool is indicated as a most suitable clothing material: for cotton, linen, and silk, having smoother surfaces, do not provide so protective an atmosphere.

Nature points to wool as the proper clothing of man, as of the lower animals, and, as is only to be expected under the circumstances, it fulfils all the conditions necessary for the preservation of health, as far as dress is concerned; it retains more warmth, while weighing less than any other material, and it allows the skin to perform those functions of transpiration, interference with which is the precursor of disease, while stoppage of them causes death, as surely as the cessation of breathing through the lungs, consequent on suffocation.

To speak now of the ventilating power of various materials. It might appear at first sight, and is, indeed, often maintained by the thoughtless, that the more impervious to air a material is the warmer it must be; but experience teaches us that this is not so. For instance, a kid glove, which can hardly be said to allow any air to pass through it, feels by no means so warm on the hand as one knitted out of wool, through which a great amount of air can pass, as may easily be seen by blowing through it. If we call the ventilating power of flannel 100, that of linen is 50, of silk 40, and of buckskin 1; but a practical comparison of the heat values of these materials shows that flannel feels decidedly the warmest when worn. Of course it may be said that it feels warmer because it is a better non-conductor, but I believe another cause for this effect may be found in its higher ventilating power. I said in a previous chapter that the skin breathes as well as the lungs, though in a less degree, and if the air is permitted to reach the skin it not only removes waste and injurious substances from the body, but it also gives oxygen to the body. This oxygen combines with the carbon in the small blood-vessels, which in countless multitudes underlie the skin, and heat is given off.

Speaking of these little blood-vessels leads me to mention another point about clothing, namely, that if clothes fit too tightly they are not so warm as those of looser make, and the reason of this is twofold. First, tight clothes press upon the little blood-vessels in the skin, and thus mechanically interfere with the circulation of the blood in them, and that hot fluid, the blood, not being permitted to flow to the skin, that organ feels the loss of its heat supply. Secondly, tight garments, permitting but little air to lie between them and the skin, do not so freely permit the interchange of those good offices of which I have spoken, between it and the air, as would looser garments.

The value of woollen clothing for occupations or sports which bring about copious perspiration is generally acknowledged, and the reason of this is that it permits the skin to dry rapidly by absorbing moisture, and does not cling to the skin wet and clammy like cotton or linen. Wet clothes conduct heat away from the body more rapidly than dry ones do, and if two men, one wearing a flannel and one a linen shirt, after a vigorous game of lawn-tennis sat down to cool, the one wearing flannel would probably suffer no ill results, while the linen-clad hero would soon feel a sudden chill, and would speedily develop all the too familiar symptoms of cold in the head, or on the chest, or of sore throat. By absorbing much of the perspiration woollen clothes prevent the chilling of the body which takes place when evaporation is too rapid.

But, besides wearing woollen during athletic sports, most men wear woollen vests, drawers, and socks – at any rate during the winter; yet our young girls, who are infinitely more in need of every advantage that clothes can offer, for the most part are allowed, even in the coldest weather, to wear cambric or cotton underclothing, in spite of the fact that most medical men are agreed that woollen underclothing is necessary in this climate.

My own opinion is that woollen should be worn not only in winter but in summer also, the only difference being in the thickness of the make and number of the garments, and I am led to believe this by the physiological facts which I have stated.

Woollen garments, if themselves kept clean, preserve the skin in a clean and healthy condition, keeping it warm in winter, and preventing chill in summer.

That irritation which sometimes follows the unaccustomed wearing of woollen next the skin is generally caused by the material being of recent manufacture or coarse quality, and in all but the rarest cases it passes off within a few days, if the practice is persevered in.

In those rare cases where irritation continues if all-wool garments are worn next the skin, a mixture of cotton and wool, as in the ordinary "shop" merinos, or of silk and wool, as in the Anglo-Indian gauze, which is perfectly smooth, may be worn.

In summer weather I believe that many cases of so-called nettle-rash, and that most painful skin disease, prickly heat, the name of which admirably describes the sensations it produces, are caused by the sudden checking of the functions of the skin, owing to the thinness of the vests worn. These cases are not often met with in medical practice, as, although extremely painful, the affections are known not to be dangerous; but I believe they are much more common than is generally thought, and privately I have met with several in the persons of young ladies who in summer wear calico next the skin . . .

There is a very prevalent idea that woollen clothing is weakening, but this is only a misapprehension of the fact that it is weakening to allow the body to be constantly overheated. Although woollen is worn, the body need not be overheated, even in summer, care being taken that the quality and quantity of the clothes is suitable to the external temperature.

To come now to the practical application of all the principles which I have endeavoured to explain in this and the preceding chapters, I recommend that the body, especially of growing girls, should be clad entirely in wool, and for this purpose I advocate the use of woollen combinations, with high necks and long sleeves. The combination garment, with the addition of woollen stockings, forms a complete and most sanitary costume, and, were it not for the sake of appearances, is all that is needed for summer wear; but other clothing is required in winter for warmth, and in summer for the sake of that tyrant appearance.

Source Excerpted from Ballin, A. S. (1885). *The science of dress in theory and practice*. London: Sampson Low, Marston, Searle, and Rivington.

Biographical note Ada S. Ballin (d. 1906) was a British philologist, and translated Muslim history and Hebrew texts. She was a lecturer to the National Health Society of London, and this reading comes from her book, which was a collection of previous lectures and articles on health issues and dress.

* * *

The Reform Dress *Amelia Bloomer* in *Dexter C. Bloomer*

… "In January or February, 1851, an article appeared editorially in the *Seneca County Courier*, Seneca Falls, N.Y., on 'Female Attire' in which the writer showed up the inconvenience, unhealthfulness and discomfort of woman's dress, and advocated a change to Turkish pantaloons and a skirt reaching a little below the knee.

"At the time, I was publishing a monthly paper in the same place devoted to the interests of woman, temperance and woman's-rights being the principal subjects. As the editor of the *Courier* was opposed to us on the woman's rights question, this article of his gave me an opportunity to score him one on having gone so far ahead of us as to advocate our wearing pantaloons, and in my next issue I noticed him and his proposed style in a half-serious, half-playful article of some length. He took up the subject again and expressed surprise that I should treat so important a matter with levity. I replied to him more seriously than before, fully indorsing and approving his views on the subject of woman's costume.

"About this time, when the readers of the *Lily* and the *Courier* were interested in and excited over the discussion, Elizabeth Smith Miller, daughter

Figure 3.3 Amelia Jenks Bloomer wearing Elizabeth Smith Miller's version of
Turkish Pantaloons and short skirt – the ensemble that became known
as the "Bloomer Costume." This image appeared in the *Illustrated
London News* in 1851, drawn from a daguerreotype by T.W. Brown of
Bloomer wearing the ensemble. From *Illustrated London News*, Vol. 19,
1851, London: William Little.

of the Hon. Gerrit Smith, of Peterboro, N.Y., appeared on the streets of our village dressed in short skirts and full Turkish trousers. She came on a visit to her cousin, Elizabeth Cady Stanton, who was then a resident of Seneca Falls. Mrs. Miller had been wearing the costume some two or three months at home and abroad. Just how she came to adopt it I have forgotten, if I ever knew. But she wore it with the full sanction and approval of her father and husband. During her father's term in congress she was in Washington, and the papers of that city described her appearance on the streets in the short costume.

"A few days after Mrs. Miller's arrival in Seneca Falls Mrs. Stanton came out in a dress made in Mrs. Miller's style. She walked our streets in a skirt that came a little above the knees, and trousers of the same material – black satin. Having had part in the discussion of the dress question, it seemed proper that I should practise as I preached, and as the *Courier* man advised; and so a few days later I, too, donned the new costume, and in the next issue of my paper announced that fact to my readers. At the outset, I had no idea of fully adopting the style; no thought of setting a fashion; no thought that my action would create an excitement throughout the civilized world, and give to the style my name and the credit due Mrs. Miller. This was all the work of the press. I stood amazed at the furor I had unwittingly caused. The New York *Tribune* contained the first notice I saw of my action. Other papers caught it up and handed it about. My exchanges all had something to say. Some praised and some blamed, some commented, and some ridiculed and condemned. 'Bloomerism,' 'Bloomerites,' and 'Bloomers' were the headings of many an article, item and squib; and finally someone – I don't know to whom I am indebted for the honor – wrote the 'Bloomer Costume,' and the name has continued to cling to the short dress in spite of my repeatedly disclaiming all right to it and giving Mrs. Miller's name as that of the originator or the first to wear such dress in public. Had she not come to us in that style, it is not probable that either Mrs. Stanton or myself would have donned it.

"As soon as it became known that I was wearing the new dress, letters came pouring in upon me by hundreds from women all over the country making inquiries about the dress and asking for patterns – showing how ready and anxious women were to throw off the burden of long, heavy skirts. It seemed as though half the letters that came to our office were for me.

"My subscription list ran up amazingly into the thousands, and the good woman's rights doctrines were thus scattered from Canada to Florida and from Maine to California. I had gotten myself into a position from which I could not recede if I had desired to do so. I therefore continued to wear the new style on all occasions, at home and abroad, at church and on the lecture platform, at fashionable parties and in my business office. I found the dress comfortable, light, easy and convenient, and well adapted to the needs of my busy life. I was pleased with it and had no desire to lay it aside, and so would not let the ridicule or censure of the press move me. For some six or eight years, or so long as I remained in active life and until the papers had ceased writing squibs at my expense, I wore no other costume. During this time I was to some extent in the lecture field, visiting in all the principal cities of the North and lecturing on temperance and woman suffrage; but at no time, on any occasion, alluding to my style of costume. I felt as much at ease in it as though I had been arrayed in the fashionable draggle skirts. In all my travels I met with nothing disagreeable or unpleasant, but was universally treated with respect and attention by both press and people wherever I appeared. Indeed, I received from the press flattering notices of my lectures. If the dress drew the crowds that came to hear me it was well. They heard the message I brought them, and it has borne abundant fruit.

"My paper had many contributions on the subject of dress and that question was for some time kept before my readers. Mrs. Stanton was a frequent contributor and ably defended the new style. She continued to wear it at home and abroad, on the lecture platform and in the social parlor, for two or three years; and then the pressure brought to bear upon her by her father and other friends was so great, that she finally yielded to their wishes and returned to long skirts.

"Lucy Stone, of the *Women's Journal*, adopted and wore the dress for many years on all occasions; but she, too, with advancing years, saw fit to return to the old style. We all felt that the dress was drawing attention from what we thought of far greater importance – the question of woman's right to better education, to a wider field of employment, to better remuneration for her labor, and to the ballot for the protection of her rights. In the minds of some people, the short dress and woman's rights were inseparably connected. With us, the dress was but an incident, and we were not willing to sacrifice greater questions to it.

. . . The costume of woman should be suited to her wants and necessities. It should conduce at once to her health, comfort, and usefulness; and, while it should not fail also to conduce to her personal adornment, it should make that end of secondary importance. I certainly need not stop to show that these conditions are not attained by the present style of woman's dress. All admit that they are not. Even those who ridicule most freely the labors of your association are ready to admit the folly and inutility of the prevailing styles.

Source Excerpted from Bloomer, D. (1975). *The life and writings of Amelia Bloomer.* New York: Shocken Books. (Original work published 1895)

Biographical note Amelia Jenks Bloomer (1818–1894) was an U.S. reformer who campaigned for temperance, and women's rights and suffrage. She was a journalist and publisher, and an early feminist writer who worked with such contemporaries as Elizabeth Cady Stanton and Susan B. Anthony. The reading is taken from the book written about her by her husband, Dexter C. Bloomer. In the book he excerpts some of her original work.

✳ ✳ ✳

The Development and Function of Clothing
Knight Dunlap

... We have now put ourselves under the necessity of answering a new question. If clothing is not conducive to modesty or to morality, but rather the contrary, why has it not disappeared? Its value as a badge has become minimized. Its protective value is not important except under conditions which do not obtain much of the time among civilized peoples. It is not conducive to health. Man could profit in comfort, and hygienically, by reducing his winter attire as woman has reduced hers, and in warm weather both sexes would be better off, hygienically, if they completely discarded raiment the greater part of the time. But still we cling to clothes as the oyster to his shell, and the police back up public opinion. Is this mere force of habit? Habit of course plays a major part, but there is another reason why we conceal our figures; a reason of vital importance to racial betterment; a reason so strong that it is possible that women may still return to long skirts and pads, and man may never emerge from his swaddlings.

The reason is to be found in sexual selection and sexual competition. We may doubt the eugenic value of sexual selection but it is nevertheless an important phenomenon in all grades of society, and profoundly influences social and individual life. Sexual competition is based on sexual selection, and is perhaps the factor of greatest importance in the preservation of certain clothing habits, once they are established.

The principles of selection are different for the male and the female, and I think the effects of this difference are recognizable in the sartorial developments of modern times. The female is evaluated primarily on the basis of what we call "beauty," which involves certain objective standards.[1] These

---

1. A more detailed discussion of these standards and their importance is given in the author's small volume on *Personal Beauty and Racial Betterment.*

standards apply to (1) form and proportion of body, (2) coloration of skin, hair, and eyes, (3) nutrition and general health, (4) coordination in movement and in posture, and (5) certain minor factors such as texture of hair and skin, form of eye, mouth and other features, quality of voice, intelligence and temperament. Other standards exist also; standards of accomplishments, of social caste, and economic circumstances, but beauty is by far the most important consideration.

Standards of beauty vary from race to race and from time to time. This is especially true of the fifth group, but applies to the others also. Standardization, however, is always on a practical basis, although the actual standards, once established tend to out-last the practical conditions on which they are based. Where no specific practical determinants exist, the characteristics peculiar to the race are important, the Chinaman preferring the normal Chinese type, the Senegambian the normal Senegambian type. The practical factors are frequently more important than they seem to be to superficial observation. Where food supplies are precarious, and the reserve fat which the woman may accumulate for the benefit of the child is of great value, preference for the obese type may be expected, as among certain African tribes of worshippers at the shrine of Aphrodite Steatopygia. Purely casual factors may from time to time become important, such as the taste for red hair which flourished for a time, supported perhaps by the rhapsodies of certain poets whose inamorata happened to be adorned with sunset hued locks. Prevailing fads have their effects, since man wants his women to be approved, if not envied, by other women. Hence the contemporary feminine penchant for pathological thinness affects temporarily the preferences of the male, although his fundamental standards are probably unchanged, and he would be relieved by the return to more normal proportions. However important may be the variable factors in beauty, the fundamental anatomical and physiological characters always have been preëminent, and for the benefit of the race we may well hope that they always will be.

Standards of sexual attractiveness of the male are characteristically different from those of the female, but are likewise on a practical basis. Certain desiderata are definitely established among Western races (although we do not refer to them as features of "beauty"), and corresponding ones obtain among other races. These are: (1) stature above the average, (2) muscular development for both strength and agility, (3) lung development for endurance, (4) racially normal features, (5) thick hair, preferably curly, and (6) aggressiveness and economic ability. Here again, cultural conditions modify the standards, and fads have their influence, but these modifications are less noticeable than in the case of the standards of female beauty. Economic ability is of course variable in form. It may be hunting and fighting ability, or ability of a herdsman or trader, or in the mechanical arts, or in politics or banditry.[2]

. . . Looking back over the history of clothing and adornment, we find a great deal which has been effective in equalizing sexual competition, reducing the competition to a less deadly level. Gloves make the hands of washerwomen and princesses look more nearly alike. Long hair permits deceitful coiffures which tend towards the uniformization of the luxuriant and the scanty locked. Hoops and bustles make Venus and the Harpy alike, below the belt. The corset squeezed all waist into an indifferent ugliness. Even long skirts, without crinoline, reduce the limbs of the goddess to somewhat the level of the knock-kneed, the bow-legged, the beanpoles, and the parlor grands. Plucking of eye-brows is another great leveler. Paint and powder, henna and kohl, parasols and fans, are among the effective union weapons in restraint of competition.

The dominant male also has not been without means and methods for the neutralization of natural defects and advantages. The camouflage of coats and trousers has already been mentioned. Robes, and other flowing and flossy garments, were early worn by men of superior social status. These garments concealed not only bandy-legs and bull-calves, but also emaciated figures and aldermanic abdomens, and were undoubtedly great aids in preventing the women of the upper class men from sighing after more Adonis-like males of the exposed lower classes. Beards have been natural concealers of faces handsome and otherwise among many races. The abolition of the beard among modern men of Western Europe and America has been of course largely due to the influence of woman, who appreciates the smooth face in personal contacts. It is not probable, however, that woman would have succeeded so soon in separating man from his natural growth of facial hair if this growth had not become so diversified that it constituted a distinct feature of individual differences. Too many men today would have beards of painful scantiness, peculiar color, or insufficient distribution on the face, if they should let them grow, to bear comparison with the well-bearded man. The beard actually became a competitive point instead of a means of concealment, before it was abolished.

The story of clothing is now practically complete. Having its primitive origin in practical protective needs, its amplification and retention under conditions which render it practically unnecessary, has been fostered by the resistance to sexual competition which is today the strongest force operating against dress reform for both sexes. Bobbed hair, the short skirt, and the peekaboo waist may be denounced in the names of sexual modesty and sexual morality, but their real objectionableness lies in their furtherance of sexual

2. The bandit has apparently been the economic type preferred by women through the ages. He is the first, and perhaps the only real "gentleman."

competition. The attack on the one-piece bathing suit may have been headed by male moralists, but its energy was supplied by women who had good reasons to distrust their ratings in a bathing beauty contest.[3]

In some respects, at least, savages have been wiser than civilized peoples. Both physical and mental hygiene demand clothing that shall not transgress the limits of protective needs. In general, we wear too much clothing, and of the wrong kind. Woman, long the worst offender, has suddenly outstripped man, both literally and in the line of progress. Man does not need the protection from cold which he claims, in winter, and in summer he needs protection only from flies, mosquitoes, and the rays of the sun in certain climates. Progress is retarded by a professed moral censorship that is really vicious. Every activity in this direction has proved itself ridiculous and obstructive. The restraint of sexual competition may be useful in certain stages of society, but this usefulness, if it occurs, soon disappears. When we shall have returned to the primitive basis of clothing, as a means of protection and nothing more, we will have lost most of our problems of sexual morality, and sexual immodesty will have disappeared along with its reflection, sexual modesty.

Source   Excerpted from Dunlap, K. (1928). The development and function of clothing. *Journal of General Psychology, 1*, 64–78. Reprinted by permission from the *Journal of General Psychology*.

Biographical note   Knight Dunlap (1875–1949) received his doctorate from Harvard University in 1903. Dunlap was appointed an instructor in psychology at Johns Hopkins University where he became Professor of Experimental Psychology and chair of the psychology department. He remained at Johns Hopkins until 1936 when he received an invitation to develop a graduate psychology program at University of California-Los Angeles. Dunlap reflects the cognitive-behavioral orientation in psychology. He served as President of the American Psychological Association and first editor of the *Journal of Comparative Psychology*, and he was a pioneer in arguing for an experimental approach to social psychology.

---

3. The aversion to bodily competition on the part of women is complicated by the fact that she fears the criticism of her competitors more than she fears the estimation of men. It is generally known that women dress for the eyes of other women, rather than for the eyes of men, who, in general do not notice the details of female attire, being much more interested in woman herself than her clothing. It is a fact also, that most women, regardless of their pulchritude or impulchritude, would rather unveil themselves completely before men than before their fellow women. They fear the criticism of other women on precisely the points of the sexual appeal to men. The corresponding inhibitions of men in respect to their own sex are far lighter, as shown by observation of their general behavior, and by their radically different conditions in gymnasiums and swimming pools for the two sexes.

Part 2

Fashioning Identity

Fashioning Identity

In this section, we focus attention on the concept of identity. What we mean by identity is an individual's roles and social positions, his or her personality, and other characteristics about him- or herself. The first two readings deal with the role of dress in the establishment of identity. These readings are followed by selections on appearance management along with presentations on the communication of specific identities. The writers come from a wide variety of disciplines with William Hazlitt (1818) being a philosopher, Mary Fry (1856) a writer concerned with dress as an expression of national identity, William I. Thomas (1908) a sociologist, Louis Flaccus (1906) a psychologist, and Grace Morton (1926) a university professor of textiles and clothing. Thomas, Flaccus, and Morton all wrote at times when their respective fields were in stages of early development. They foresaw the connections between dress and its potential as an area of social-science research.

Establishing Identity

William Hazlitt (1818) addresses the question of the function of fashion in his own time period. He describes fashion as living only in a "giddy round of constant innovation and restless vanity" (p. 52), defining it as a process of constant superficial change. Hazlitt contends "dress is the great secret of address" (p. 55). Hazlitt views participation in fashion as expensive and confined to the wealthier class in communicating an individual's station in life. Hazlitt criticizes fashion as wasteful, therefore, having no purposes except to induce change. He claims that fashion is losing its power because it allows class distinction to be masked.

Hazlitt (1818) says that fashion became a "mere affectation on one side, and gradually ceased to be made a matter of aristocratic assumption on the other" (p. 54). In this argument, fashion is a moral issue. Beauty and truth are virtue, and therefore, once fashion becomes mere imitation, anyone, even the lowest, can assume "airs and graces of pretended superiority" (p. 56). To Hazlitt, increased participation in the fashion system removes the ability to distinguish class distinctions and refinement. Dress is no longer a matter of taste and beauty, or a way to display accomplishment and virtue.

Mary Fry (1856) calls for the development of a national costume in a time when many prominent U.S. citizens were following European fashions, and when the French apparel industry was seen as providing fashion leaders. According to Fry, this national costume should be based on Christian ideals and reflect U.S. democratic beliefs. She states that Americans should stop trying to copy or emulate a style of life that is, in her view, un-American. Money should not be spent wastefully on extravagant fashion, but should support other family needs. Fry's general ideas for an American national costume include clothing that is "at once neat, comfortable, and elegant, and which might be regarded by other nations as something of an index to their [American] professed democratic principles" (p. 736). According to Fry, fashion conflicts with democracy, and Americans should not rely upon England and France for fashion leadership, or send money to them. She strongly advocated that Americans should keep that money at home. Her use of the term costume, used synonymously with "clothing," fits with ours. Fry's use is also historically consistent with the national-costume or folk-dress movement in the nineteenth century.

William I. Thomas (1908) begins his discussion by reflecting on humans as primarily unadorned in comparison to other animals in the natural world. He argues that, over time, humans have been able to use objects to adorn themselves. He labels these objects as ornament, and says that they are used to communicate the following aspects of identity – sexual attractiveness, power, and sex. He distinguishes clothing from ornament and suggests that clothing was primarily protective worn in cold climates while ornament was worn in the tropics. According to Thomas, the habit of wearing only ornament gradually changed to wearing clothing to cover the entire body. His clear distinction between ornament and clothing does not coincide with the body-modification and body-supplement ideas that we presented in defining dress.

Thomas (1908) observes that unlike animals that cannot change their feathers or fur, humans adopt and discard clothing styles. Their ability to make rapid style changes communicates economic standing, or their ability to engage in what Veblen (1894, 1899) labeled "conspicuous waste" (p. 166). Thomas explains gender differences in dress by noting that men appear to have given up wearing ornament and that women appear to desire and specialize in wearing it. As a result, women's appearance does not reflect their individual identities but rather symbolizes the household. In addition, the communication of women's identities is further subjugated by the fashion industry. In Thomas's words, "women do not wear what they want . . . The people who supply them also control them" (p. 69). In taking a stand to raise women's position in society at this time, Thomas contends that this situation "leaves society short-handed and the struggle for life harder and uglier than it would be if women operated in it as the substantial and superior creature which nature made her" (p. 70).

Appearance Management

In attempting to take a scientific approach to the study of clothing, Louis Flaccus (1906) reviews the survey results of a questionnaire originally developed by G. Stanley Hall in 1905. Hall designed the survey to assess the feelings and opinions of college-aged females about their use of clothing and he refers only to garments. Flaccus groups Hall's findings into three broad categories – one dealing with minor matters or "psychological tidbits," one dealing with how clothing impacts the individual, and the third dealing with how clothing impacts relationships with others. Providing only a description of the findings and limited analysis, he concludes that there is much to be done to understand the relationship between individuals and their clothing. In 1906, he outlines those issues or problems he believes about clothing and mental life that may undergo investigation. Flaccus clearly believes that the psychology of clothes is important. He states that because the field of psychology is still developing, scientific research on the topic may be limited. He makes thoughtful recommendations for supplementing Hall's earlier research and "suggests several problems of a very promising kind" (1906 p. 82) that reflect questions and issues we continue to investigate.

Two decades later, in her short essay on the psychology of dress, Grace Morton (1926) echoes Flaccus' (1906) recognition that the psychology of clothing is a significant area of study. As professor of clothing and textiles, she acknowledges the impact of what we call appearance management on the individual. She points out that the clothes we wear determine "how much we go into society, the places we go to, the exercises we take" (p. 484). She also notes that the right clothes "help us to express the best in ourselves and are a means of giving pleasure to those about us" (p. 484). Morton remarks on the need for scientific studies on the relationships between the aesthetics of dress and personality. She argues that such research will be "revolution-izing" (p. 66) in the teaching of clothing, creating a new vocation of clothing advisor, and elevating clothing selection from an intuition base to a scientific base. Her ideas about a clothing advisor were ahead of her time, foreseeing the profession of wardrobe consultant that emerged in the late twentieth century and the introduction of such books as John Molloy's *Dress for Success* (1975).

Reference

Molloy, J.T. (1975). *Dress for success*. New York: P.H. Wyden.

4

Establishing Identity

On Fashion *William Hazlitt*

Fashion is an odd jumble of contradictions, of sympathies and antipathies. It exists only by its being participated among a certain number of persons, and its essence is destroyed by being communicated to a greater number. It is a continual struggle between "the great vulgar and the small" to get the start of or keep up with each other in the race of appearances, by an adoption on the part of the one of such external and fantastic symbols as strike the attention and excite the envy or admiration of the beholder, and which are no sooner made known and exposed to public view for this purpose, than they are successfully copied by the multitude, the slavish herd of imitators, who do not wish to be behind-hand with their betters in outward show and pretensions, and which then sink, without any farther notice, into disrepute and contempt. Thus fashion lives only in a perpetual round of giddy innovation and restless vanity. To be old-fashioned is the greatest crime a coat or a hat can by guilty of. To look like nobody else is a sufficiently mortifying reflection; to be in danger of being mistaken for one of the rabble is worse. Fashion constantly begins and ends in the two things it abhors most, singularity and vulgarity. It is the perpetual setting up and disowning a certain standard of taste, elegance, and refinement, which has no other foundation or authority than that it is the prevailing distinction of the moment, which was yesterday ridiculous from its being new, and to-morrow will be odious from its being common. It is one of the most slight and insignificant of all things. It cannot be lasting, for it depends on the constant change and shifting of its own harlequin disguises; it cannot be sterling, for, if it were, it could not depend on the breath of caprice; it must be superficial, to produce its immediate effect on the gaping crowd; and frivolous, to admit of its being assumed at pleasure by the numbers of those who affect, by being in the fashion, to be distinguished from the rest of the world. It is not anything in itself, nor the sign of any thing but the folly and vanity of those who rely upon it as their greatest pride and ornament. It takes the firmest hold of the most flimsy and narrow minds, of those whose emptiness conceives of nothing excellent but what is thought so by others, and whose self-conceit makes

Figure 4.1 Dressed in the height of fashion for the theater, 1818. According to
Hazlitt, it is impossible to tell from her dress if this young woman is of
"first quality" or if she is "no better than" an inexperienced, uneducated,
common country or servant girl pretending to be of a higher status.
Evening dress, 1818 from *Repository of Arts, Literature, Commerce,
Manufactures, Fashions and Politics*, 1818, London: Rudolf Ackermann.
The illustration was found in *Ackermann's Costume Plates: Women's
Fashions in England, 1818–1828* (p. 2, 8), by S. Blum, 1978, New York:
Dover Publications.

them willing to confine the opinion of all excellence to themselves and those like them. That which is true or beautiful in itself, is not the less so for standing alone. That which is good for anything, is the better for being more widely diffused. But fashion is the abortive issue of vain ostentation and exclusive egotism: it is haughty, trifling, affected, servile, despotic, mean, and ambitious, precise and fantastical, all in a breath – tied to no rule, and bound to conform to every whim of the minute. "The fashion of an hour old mocks the wearer." It is a sublimated essence of levity, caprice, vanity, extravagance, idleness, and selfishness. It thinks of nothing but not being contaminated by vulgar use, and winds and doubles like a hare, and betakes itself to the most paltry shifts to avoid being overtaken by the common hunt that are always in full chase after it. It contrives to keep up its fastidious pretensions, not by the difficulty of the attainment, but by the rapidity and evanescent nature of the changes. It is a sort of conventional badge, or understood passport into select circles, which must still be varying (like the water-mark in bank-notes) not to be counterfeited by those without the pale of fashionable society; for to make the test of admission to all the privileges of that refined and volatile atmosphere depend on any real merit or extraordinary accomplishment, would exclude too many of the pert, the dull, the ignorant, too many shallow, upstart, and self-admiring pretenders, to enable the few that passed muster to keep one another in any tolerable countenance. If it were the fashion, for instance, to be distinguished for virtue, it would be difficult to set or follow the example; but then this would confine the pretension to a small number, (not the most fashionable part of the community), and would carry a very singular air with it. Or if excellence in any art or science were made the standard of fashion, this would also effectually prevent vulgar imitation, but then it would equally prevent fashionable impertinence. There would be an obscure circle of *virtù* as well as virtue, drawn within the established circle of fashion, a little province of a mighty empire – the example of honesty would spread slowly, and learning would still have to boast of a respectable minority. But of what use would such uncourtly and out-of-the-way accomplishments be to the great and noble, the rich and the fair, without any of the *éclat*, the noise and nonsense which belong to that which is followed and admired by all the world alike? The real and solid will never do for the current coin, the common wear and tear of foppery and fashion. It must be the meretricious, the showy, the outwardly fine, and intrinsically worthless – that which lies within the reach of the most indolent affectation, that which can be put on or off at the suggestion of the most wilful caprice, and for which, through all its fluctuations, no mortal reason can be given, but that it is the newest absurdity in vogue! . . .

. . . What shews the worthlessness of mere fashion is, to see how easily this vain and boasted distinction is assumed, when the restraints of decency or circumstances are once removed, by the most uninformed and commonest of the people. I know an undertaker that is the greatest prig in the streets of London, and an Aldermanbury haberdasher, that has the most military strut of any lounger in Bond-street or St. James's. We may, at any time, raise a regiment of fops from the same number of fools, who have vanity enough to be intoxicated with the smartness of their appearance, and not sense enough to be ashamed of themselves. Everyone remembers the story in Peregrine Pickle, of the strolling gipsy that he picked up in spite, had well scoured, and introduced her into genteel company, where she met with great applause, till she got into a passion by seeing a fine lady cheat at cards, rapped out a volley of oaths, and let nature get the better of art. Dress is the great secret of address. Clothes and confidence will set anybody up in the trade of modish accomplishment. Look at the two classes of well-dressed females whom we see at the play-house, in the boxes. Both are equally dressed in the height of the fashion, both are *rouged*, and wear their neck and arms bare – both have the same conscious, haughty, theatrical air – the same toss of the head, the same stoop in the shoulders, with all the grace that arises from a perfect freedom from embarrassment, and all the fascination that rises from a systematic disdain of formal prudery – the same pretence and jargon of fashionable conversation – the same mimicry of tones and phrases – the same "lisping, and ambling, and painting, and nicknaming of Heaven's creatures"; the same every thing but real propriety of behaviour, and real refinement of sentiment. In all the externals, they are as like as the reflection in the looking-glass. The only difference between the woman of fashion and the woman of pleasure is, that the one *is* what the other only *seems to be*; and yet, the victims of dissipation who thus rival and almost outshine women of the first quality in all the blaze, and pride, and glitter of shew and fashion, are, in general, no better that a set of raw, uneducated, inexperienced country girls, or awkward, coarse-fisted servant maids who require no other apprenticeship or qualification to be on a level with persons of the highest distinction in society, in all the brilliancy and elegance of outward appearance, than that they have forfeited its common privileges, and every title to respect in reality. The truth is, that real virtue, beauty, or understanding, are the same, whether "in a high or low degree"; and the airs and graces of pretended superiority over these which the highest classes give themselves, from mere frivolous and external accomplishments, are easily imitated, with provoking success, by the lowest, whenever they *dare* . . .

Source Excerpted from Hazlitt, W. (1818). On fashion. *The Edinburgh Magazine.*

Biographical note   William Hazlitt (1778–1830) was an English writer. As the son of a Unitarian preacher who supported the American revolution, his childhood was spent in Ireland and North America until the age of nine. In his late twenties, he studied painting, worked as a portrait painter, lectured on philosophy, and produced his first book. He later worked as a parliamentary reporter, an art, literary and theater critic, and biographer. His essays are known for his humanist philosophy.

* * *

Let Us Have a National Costume *Mary E. Fry*

A recent writer closes an article on "Licentiousness in the Fine Arts" with these words: "Let us have a Christian art – if need be, an American Christian art – and if the great artistic world contemn us, we can pity it till it learns better." To this we heartily respond, and beg leave to add, Let us have a *Christian costume*, and, if need be, an *American Christian costume*; and if the fashionable world at Paris and elsewhere sneer at us, we ought to be able to bear it till they shall have learned to imitate us.

If, as a nation, we are in some danger of marring our innate modesty while taking the corrupt art of the old world, especially European art, for our mode, no more can we go on imitating the costume and manners of one of the most corrupt cities of the old world without a corresponding loss in our morality and native good taste. Costume, it is true, is no more identical with morals than taste is, yet one may and greatly does influence the other, as, for instance, no one would expect to find an immodest costume on a Christian woman of refined taste, any more than he would look for a neat, modest, and elegant attire on a courtesan.

But what *is* costume? Webster defines it to be "an established mode of dress." According to this definition, then, nothing of the kind had existed among us during the last one hundred and fifty years; for in a period of less than one hundred years, from 1760 to 1850, we find more than twenty of the most distinct fashions in existence, to say not one word of the numberless *variations* of these fashions during the same time. Perhaps most of our women have a dim recollection of reading somewhere of such a thing as Japanese, Spanish, or Italian costume for females; well, we assure them no historian or chronicler of veracity will ever venture to tell the world what is the *national* costume of American, English, or French ladies. He might, indeed, go so far as to say, that the women of these countries wore certain articles of dress called bonnets, hats, shawls, cloaks, mantillas, and gowns, of every imaginable size, shape, color, and material; but a more definite description he could not venture on. And he might add, as an incontrovertible truth, that, as a general thing, in

Figure 4.2 Fry's call for a national American dress that eschewed French and
British fashions was taken up by many women in the Unites States.
This version was shown over thirty years later at the Chicago World's
Fair, recommended by the Executive Board of the Council of Women of
the United States and their standing Committee on Dress. They argued
that this style of walking gown would be the most comfortable and
practical for visiting the Fair, and hoped that this variation of the
"American Costume" could become an accepted fashion and regarded
as beautiful dress for women. Mrs. Annie Jenness Miller's "American
Costume" from Dress Reform at the World's Fair (p. 313), in *The Review
of Reviews*, 7 (January–June), 1893, New York: The Review of Reviews.

matters of dress the French took the lead, and the rest of the enlightened world, regardless of health, climate, comfort, or even modesty, acquiesced in all humility . . .

. . . But all must see that it is at war with our form of government, to be dependent on the nod of a foreign aristocracy for the form and material of our dress; and in the abstract – not so abstractly either – it is at war with national prosperity. For an extravagant, foreign costume, presupposes a corresponding style of living, both of which are a sure and speedy means for the depletion of either a private or public treasury. And during the process of this depletion we must take into account how often and sorely peace and justice are trampled under foot; for be the extravagance whatever it may, it is the bone and sinew of the land – the laboring masses – who must apply the means for its gratification. We will not stop to say how much the national prosperity has advanced since the discovery of gold in California; but it is surely of little avail to the country that one vessel after another arrives at New York laden with its million, or half-million of gold dust, if an equivalent sum is as often shipped to Europe to pay for foreign goods, which the country could well dispense with, if our women had a little more of the spirit of the elder Mrs. Adams.

If anyone has doubts as to the increasing extravagance of costume among American women, he has only to glance carefully over the statistical tables of imports, to convince himself that costly foreign goods form something more than moderate items in the list. Indeed, to such a degree of insanity – one can call it nothing else – have a class of American women arrived, that it is asserted that merchants and milliners find it no easy matter to procure goods sufficiently high-priced to suit their taste (?) and purses; they, to their shame and folly be it said, being more particular about the price than the quality. American women at Paris, and other places, are known to purchase articles of dress at prices which would startle a duchess, whose annual income alone amounts to more than the entire fortune of some of these would-be aristocrats. No wonder crashing, ruinous failures follow in the footsteps of such inexcusable imbecility – no wonder if these dear Europeans point their fingers at us, and ask sneeringly among themselves, to what quarter of the globe we have cast our former re-publican spirit. Why, it is not so very many years ago since our fathers fought, and bled, and died, and *conquered* in the struggle to secure an independent government for us; and our mothers, scorning the luxuries of the old world, spun and wove, and cut and made the clothing for their entire household; have their children degenerated *so soon*? Is it true that Americans, and especially American women, have already become so incompetent, so utterly wanting in the article of ingenuity, that they can not even contrive to model for themselves a costume at once neat, comfortable, and elegant; and which might be regarded by other nations as something of an index to their professed democratic principles?. . .

. . . But even greater than the necessity which exists for reform in dress – and which in fact must precede it – is the want of a spirit of independence, which will enable Americans to be more emphatically *themselves*; for it is folly to deny that this grand emblem of nationality is painfully wanting in the so-called "society," who claim the privilege of giving tone to manners and morals. It is plain to every observer, that if the mass of our people were as deficient in patriotism as this exclusive class, our form of government would crumble to dust in a twinkling. And, so long as the "exclusive few" continue to spend their energies in making as close an imitation to European life as their means and position will allow, it is useless to expect they will exert themselves much in behalf of the elevation of their own countrymen. Happily enough, however, the country can tolerably well dispense with them; for it is the intelligent, independent, and patriotic masses who are the pillars upholding government, and who alone give a practical voice to religion and politics, to morals and customs.

. . . For we hold that individual culture must, to a great extent, precede all permanent elevation of the masses; there may, indeed, be individual culture without this elevation of the whole, but most assuredly no permanent elevation of the mass without the exclusive culture of the individual. Nor need this again be the least discouragement, but rather otherwise as it leaves each woman free to act, speak, and improve herself for whatever her own judgment dictates to be her proper sphere; provided, always, that at no time she steps beyond the bounds of propriety, religion, and her domestic duties. For every true woman is a law unto herself, and needs not that the public should prescribe rules for the regulation of her life, any more than for the expense or mode of her wardrobe; the most she needs is a word of encouragement to keep her in that path of duty, which she has already marked out for herself. And every true woman can, ought, and will do something for her own individual culture and elevation, independently of what society expects and academic halls prescribe. And if at any time she be lacking in motive to exertion, she has but to bear in mind who plucked the apple, and what the consequences have been; she will then soon learn that, as through her man fell, so also through her must she rise again to his former estate. But before she can ever achieve this restoration, she has first to learn more thoroughly for herself, that as an intellectual being, an immortal soul, the food for her mind is of infinitely more importance that the raiment for her body, and the intelligent mastery and guidance of her own spirit, worth ten thousand triumphs in a fleeting world of fashion.

Source Excerpted from Fry, M.E. (1856). Let us have a national costume. *The Ladies' Repository*, 735–738.

Biographical note Mary Fry was a regular contributor to *The Ladies' Repository*, a monthly periodical dedicated to literature, arts, and religion, published during the nineteenth century. In the mid-1800s, she published eleven articles in *The Ladies' Repository*, with topics that ranged from dress to writing manuscripts for publications.

✳ ✳ ✳

The Psychology of Woman's Dress *William I. Thomas*

The advances which modern life has made over savagery are represented at some points by a very thin line. Old practices are refined, the old forms are presented with slightly different coloring and arrangement, and the emphasis is placed at different points, but we do not get clean away from the old patterns. Savage life, in its turn, borders very close on the animal, and sociology and psychology must continually go back to the simpler conditions of animal life to pick up the cue. Man is naturally one of the most unadorned of animals, without brilliant appearance or natural glitter, with no plumage, no spots or stripes, no naturally sweet voice, no attractive odor, and no graceful antics. But, thanks to his hands, he has the power of collecting brilliant objects and attaching them to his person, and he thus becomes a rival in radiance of the animals and flowers . . .

. . . Rapid rotation style is a device to attract attention not known to animal life and not systematically used in the Orient. The woman of the Far East uses expensive and attractive materials, but she wears them, as she does jewels, for a long period. Among Occidental women the discarding of dress is not only seasonal but, if it can be afforded, diurnal. The constant change is not only striking in itself, but the economic ability to make it distinguish both the woman and the man whom she represents. What Mr. Veblen happily terms "conspicuous waste" is a means of distinction which the masses are not in a position to copy.

Personal display is dangerous ground for woman, since it involves disgust in the spectator when overdone, and she would never be bold enough to carry it to such outspoken lengths if she were not operating in a flock. She is timid about emphasizing herself except as one of a flock, but she is anxious for all the conspicuousness she can get in the flock, and is above all concerned to be a member of the most distinguished flock. At this point she shows some independence of man and almost loses sight of him (after marriage, at least) in her interest in outstripping other women. Men would prefer her more simply dressed; but this is her game – indeed, it is almost her business.

As society advances there is a tendency in man to give up ornament and in woman to take on more of it. This is not because man is naturally less inclined to display, but because he has undergone a great reform in his habits, the greatest perhaps in the history of the world. Primitive man was pugnacious, unsocial, ostentatious, and lazy, but capable, crafty, and masterfuly – our true adventurer, but endowed with an inventive imagination and capable of splendid bursts of energy. This was the wild-oats period of the race, and its vestiges are still seen in the gamester, the artist, the wild youth, and the dissipated husband.

But when man exhausted the game which had been his principal pursuit and began to take up the settled manufacturing and agricultural interests which had been chiefly developed by woman, and to buy and sell, he brought with him more ingenuity than woman had ever developed, a freer movement, a greater power of organization, and at the same time less domestic responsibility, and he gradually transferred some of his interest in the pursuit of game to the pursuit of business. But business lies, so to speak, outside the region of appearances. It is primarily a matter of judgment, efficiency, and energy, and if a man has efficiency and wealth in abundance he is attractive enough without ornament. No one ever completely loses an interest in bright objects, but business men take advantage of this fact to display their goods, not their persons. The color sense and the sexual interest are recognized in the display, wrapping, and advertising of wares. The glaring billboard and the beautiful lady on the cigar-box saturate the goods with color and sex, and we buy them on that basis. But pretentiously housed business and a handsomely gowned wife are also capital advertisements; they are signs of business success, and "nothing succeeds like success." . . .

. . . The dress of woman has, in fact, become so incorporated in business that, as Sir Henry Maine has pointed out, the greatest calamity which could be conceived as befalling great populations would be, not a sanguinary war, a desolating famine, or a deadly epidemic, but a revolution in fashion under which "women should dress, as men practically do, in one material of one color. There are many flourishing and opulent cities in Europe and America which would be condemned by it to bankruptcy or starvation, and it would be worse than a famine or pestilence in China, India, and Japan." That is to say, any great change in our industrial system must be gradual not to be calamitous.

But, while woman's demands occupy so large a place in the industrial world, it is noticeable that she is herself only a pawn in the industrial game played by man. Her individual possessor uses her as a symbol of his wealth, and the captains of industry make her and her changeable and expensive fashions the occasion of a market for the costly and changeable objects which fashionable habits force her to accept. New fashions are not always beautiful; they are even often ugly, and women know it: but they embrace changes as frequent and as radical as the ingenuity of the mode makers can devise. Women do not wear what they want, but what the manufacturers and trades-people want them to want. The people who supply them also control them.

This does not, however, alter the fact that the general tone and pace of social life are deeply influenced by woman's emphasis of finery and form. There is an old story of a lady who purchased a pair of brass andirons and then by degrees persuaded her husband to refurnish the whole house to match them. Just so, when silks and furs and gems and lace and the unminted gold are attached to the person of woman, it follows also that the household and the world in which she moves are transformed to harmonize with her showy taste and appearance. Beginning with the rugs, tapestry, porcelain, silver plate, fine linen, and the rich and gaudy furnishings of the home, the factitious personality of woman pervades and bedizens everything. The baffling array of silver at the twelve-course dinner and the costly box at the costly opera are equally a part of woman's dress. This situation is the despair of men, but it is "society."

The effect of this situation on the character of woman is altogether bad. One interest expels another or prevents its development. The proverbially hollow mind of the very beautiful woman is not due to the exhaustion of nature's resources on her exterior, but to the fact that her attention is so bound up with the expression of her own charm that it stops with that. And the homely woman who competes with her has a still more absorbing problem. The foolish and disrespectful customs of courtesy which men practise toward women are also a product of woman's dress, and tend to keep her helpless in mind and body. The helplessness involved in lacing, high heels, undivided skirts, and other impedimenta of women has a certain charm in the eyes of man. Their helplessness shows him off better by giving freer play to his protective and masterful instincts. It is his heroic opportunity since the disappearance of large game and in the "piping times of peace." To flatter this disposition of man, woman therefore assumes even greater helplessness than she possesses, and the most romantic periods in history are those characterized by tight lacing and purposive fainting.

The rôle of "half angel and half bird" is a pretty one, if you can look at it in that way; but it denatures woman, makes her a thing instead of a person, a fact of the environment and an object of man's manipulation instead of an agent for transforming the world. It leaves society short-handed and the struggle for life harder and uglier than it would be if woman operated in it as the substantial and superior creature which nature made her. We have a machine-made civilization which has introduced class inequalities, hatred, and suffering unknown in savagery or barbarism. We are wealthy but not humanized. Man is pursuing business on the same pitiless principle that he formerly pursued game. Women have a base of maternal feeling that makes them more social than man, and if the economic value of the superfluity of their dress and the energy and attention they waste in following the fashions were devoted to humanistic enterprises we should be in a fair way to add the elements lacking to make our machine system a civilization. But there is no use trying to talk fashions down. The change will come gradually, as women become more intelligent and independent and of themselves "experience the expulsive power of a new affection."

Source Excerpted from Thomas, W.I. (1908). The psychology of women's dress. *The American Magazine, 67,* 66–72.

Biographical note William I. Thomas (1863–1947) was an American sociologist and social psychologist, whose fields of study included cultural change and personality development. He taught sociology at the University of Chicago (1894–1918), the New School for Social Research (1923–1928), and Harvard University (1936–1937).

5

Appearance Management

Remarks on the Psychology of Clothes *Louis W. Flaccus*

. . . No one, I think, will deny the general statement that clothes have a marked effect upon our mental life. But it is one thing to make a broad statement of this sort, and quite another thing to ground it scientifically, and to define with some approach to accuracy and thoroughness the nature of this effect and some of its causes.

The problem at hand shares with many others which have been recently taken up certain difficulties in the way of a scientifically accredited discussion. The following is the crux of the matter. Certain mental states are so complex and of so subtle an origin that they cannot be dealt with analytically with any measure of success by the current methods of psychology. The less a chance for physiological and experimental work, the greater the difficulty. Thus, while we have some excellent papers on the feeling-tone of sounds and colours and the aesthetic value of certain simple forms, we have much wild theorizing on such complex matters as the nature of evanescent aesthetic emotions of the total affective state of consciousness during the appreciation of a tragedy. The psychology of the crowd, of the weather, the study of ideals, etc. – these are all interesting problems. The psychical effect may be traced; the demand for an explanation is justifiable; we must, however, admit that this demand overtaxes the present resources of psychology. To hope that psychology will ever be able to give a scientific formulation of all that stirs in the depths of consciousness is to be unduly optimistic. There are, I believe, certain experiences so extremely subjective that they do not admit even of the preliminary process of fixation.

Luckily for us, the problem of the effect of clothes on the psychical life is not hopelessly insoluble, although in some of its aspects it is on the ragged edge of scientific analysis. There are what the Germans call Anhaltspunkte. Certain effects are indirectly traceable to physiological factors – skin sensations of pressure, contact, temperature, etc. – others show the simplest routine working of association of ideas. The interest there lies solely in bringing out the facts of connection. Much of the material then comes under the usual rubrics of psychology. When physiological clues are not to be had and psychological terminology proves insufficient, nothing can be attempted beyond a few tentative suggestions.

. . . It is, perhaps, hardly serviceable to sum up and draw conclusions from what are frankly acknowledged to be suggestions of an unsystematic kind, based on very limited material. Attention has at least been drawn to two factors in the far-reaching effect of clothes on the mental life.

1. *Simple*: such as any ordinary psychology must take account of.
2. *Complex*: (a) such as are found in subtle personal reactions; (b) such as are found in the operation of standards of group-judgment.

This study may be supplemented in many ways, and it is my purpose to outline very briefly what is needed towards such supplementation and to suggest several problems of a very promising kind.

1. Simple psychological experiments with a view towards ascertaining the sense-factors in the psychological effects of clothes.
2. A study of more complex factors, such as emotional displacements, aesthetic judgments, changes in personality.
3. Studies in abnormal psychology with a view towards connecting any changes in the clothes-consciousness with the well-known insane delusions in the body-consciousness.
4. A study of sex-differences. This should prove one of the most fruitful lines of investigation.
5. A study of differences due to age, station, interest, etc. A questionnaire like the one discussed does not give the whole story. Generalizations would be one-sided. On the other hand the peculiar part clothes play in the consciousness of actors or tailors or uniformed officials should be noted and investigated. At this point attention might be drawn to the investigation of clothes as steadying forces or regenerative agencies of a social kind, as in reform schools or as facilitating social organization (badges, insignia, uniforms).
6. A study of clothes from the point of view of social psychology. This would mean an exhaustive analysis of group-estimates, group-standards, etc.
7. An account of social symbolism in dress and its relation to emotional states. This would mean a discussion of membership insignia, national costumes, characteristic colors and styles, mourning and bridal costumes, professional cuts, etc. Valuable hints have been thrown out on these points by H. Schurtz, Urgeschichte der Kultur.
8. An anthropological account of dress and ornament (cf. H. Schurtz, Grundzüge einer Philosophie der Tracht).

9.   An adequate historico-psychological account of costumes, fashion, etc.
10. A genetic account of clothing with the view towards a genetic theory. The latter can be done only on the basis of a vast array of materials, but should prove very valuable, since it in turn would give us the key to many curious facts.

It is for the purpose of stimulating an investigation of the many problems instanced that these suggestions on the very complex interplay of psychological effects of clothing are set forth.

Source   Excerpted from Flaccus, L.W. (1906). Remarks on the psychology of clothes. *The Pedagogical Seminary, 13,* 61–83.

Biographical note   Louis Flaccus (1880–1953) received a doctorate from Harvard in 1904. He taught philosophy at the University of Pennsylvania.

* * *

Psychology of Dress *Grace Margaret Morton*

Undoubtedly there are a few exceptional people to whom clothes mean very little aside from efficiency and who, in spite of boasted indifference to appearance, do "arrive" professionally. But for the vast majority of the human race, clothes play a large part in making for happiness and success. Even children are susceptible to the effect of clothes. Margaret Story writes of an experiment tried out in one of our city slums. A ragged, dirty child from the street was taken to a welfare home. She was scrubbed, shampooed, and dressed in clean, attractive clothes. The transformation was startling. She was changed almost immediately from a listless, broken-spirit child to a self-respecting and well-mannered little lady.

Clothes help to make us self-confident, self-respecting, jolly, free, or they may make us self-conscious, shy, sensitive, restrained. They determine how much we go into society, the places we go, the exercises we take. They help us to get jobs and to hold them, to miss them and to lose them.

Clothes that are suitable, appropriate, and beautiful help us to express the best in ourselves and are a means of giving pleasure to those about us. Being well dressed is an evidence of good taste. A passage from Ruskin reads something like this: "What you like determines what you are." Another old adage may be paraphrased thus: "The way you look speaks so loud I cannot hear what you say." Clothes, then, make or mar us. They may enhance our personality or be so conspicuous as to subordinate us to them, or they may be just ordinary, nondescript, characterless. I am thinking of a young teacher of my acquaintance – a very sedate, earnest, shy, little soul with very light bobbed hair, who wore when I first knew her a tan felt hat and dark blue twill frock with red trimming. I must confess this little lady did not impress me greatly then. Some months later, after a careful study of clothes, she appeared in a becoming black velvet hat and a dress of green-blue charmeen with frills of soft green and violet crepe. You would not believe till you could see the charm these new clothes brought out. Her hair was soft and golden, her eyes were deep blue, and her complexion lovely. The shyness, the reserve, the mousiness were gone. She was a distinct personality, dainty, demure, peppy, quite convincing.

Since the beginning of time women have consciously or unconsciously dressed to suit their types, but it has remained for this scientific era to classify personality and to discover those principles of line, color, and materials which best express each personality.

Considered from a purely anatomical standpoint, there are short stout and tall stout people, thin angular ones, and the rest. Especially must be remembered those with special difficulties of proportions which call for an application of that psychological principle requiring that we make something interesting happen to carry the eye away from the particular difficulty we wish to conceal.

A study of the spiritual and mental characteristics of women reveals two outstanding different classes – the one stately, dramatic, striking, forceful; and the other dainty, petite, demure, naïve. Seldom do we find a perfect example of either type. Most of us are combinations, but nearly all of us have tendencies toward one or the other big class. Almost invariably the most becoming costumes in any wardrobe whether chosen deliberately or intuitively do show such qualities of structure, color, and texture as to verify the claim that dressing to suit one's type is based on scientific principles.

Such personality study together with a knowledge of the psychology of design, color, and texture, so essential to its use, is revolutionizing the teaching of clothing, opening up a new vocation, that of clothing advisor, and lifting clothing selection from the realm of the intangible based on intuition and personal bias to the dignity of a tangible art with a scientific basis.

Source Morton, G. (1926). Psychology of dress. *Journal of Home Economics, 18*, 484–486. Used by permission from the Association of Family and Consumer Sciences-*Journal of Home Economics.*

Biographical note Grace Margaret Morton (d. 1943) was a professor of textiles and clothing at the University of Nebraska. Her work includes a book on costume selection. Her background was in art.

Part 3

The "F" Word

The "F" Word

We borrowed the title of this section, "The 'F' Word," from Valerie Steele's 1991 article.[1] In it, she captures the controversy among academics that surrounds the topic of fashion, citing everything from disdain to silence and embarrassment. Generally, everyone agrees that fashion involves change. Our selections examine fashion as a change agent along with offering explanations for why dress changes. Writers provide methods to predict fashion change and discuss participation in fashion as collective behavior as well as consumer behavior. We chose authors with ideas that continue to interest contemporary fashion researchers. In this section, the writers come from the disciplines of anthropology, biology, sociology, psychology, art history, theater, and economics.

Fashion as Change

George Darwin (1872) in his attempt to explain change proposes that the development of dress parallels the evolution of species, borrowing heavily from the evolutionary theory of his father, Charles Darwin. He uses the term dress to refer to garments and accessories (such as hats or boots) and defines fashion as the "love of novelty and the extraordinary tendency which men have to exaggerate any peculiarity" (p. 410). He notes "the law of progress holds good in dress and forms blend into one another with almost complete continuity" (p. 410). By the process of natural selection, those forms of dress that are not beneficial disappear and those that serve some function remain. In addition to the operation of the laws of progress and natural selection, fashion plays an important role in the development of dress. However, the process of selection in dress is not because of sexual selection, but rather because of fashion selection.

According to Darwin (1872), participation in fashion is "a mark of good station in life" (p. 410), whereby he adds an element of status to the process of fashion selection. As proof of the existence of progress in both dress and

1. Steele, V. (1991). The "F" word. *Lingua Franca, 2,* 16–20.

animals, Darwin posits "remnants of former stages of development survive to a later stage, and thus preserve a tattered record of the history of their evolution" (p. 410). These archaic remnants are present in two forms: "Some parts of the dress have been fostered and exaggerated by the selection of fashion, and are then retained and crystallized" even though their use is gone; and "[p]arts originally useful . . . have been handed down in an atrophied condition" (p. 410). He notes that it is not just in dress that one can find these remnants, but also in any quotidian object. According to Darwin, archaic forms are most often retained in ceremonial or ritual dress, such as court dress, formal evening clothes, or uniforms.

Herbert Spencer (1896), although not directly discussing fashion per se, also uses an evolutionary explanation for the change and development of body modifications and supplements. He uses dress, clothing, and ornament inconsistently but is clearly concerned with the topic of dressing the body and its importance from a sociological perspective. According to Spencer, change in dress (our term) is a sequential process of becoming civilized. Spencer, in attempting to explain contemporaneous uses of clothing and the profusion of decorative ornament, contends that one must first understand their origins or roots in primitive cultures. Spencer labels early forms of clothing as trophies. Because human beings dominate the animal world, trophies result as the spoils of the hunt. As marks of honor, trophies evolve into badges to designate status or rank in a social situation. Just as badges derive from trophies, ornament evolves from badges, for an ornament symbolically represents the original badge. To Spencer, clothing has the same capabilities as a badge in symbolically designating prestige and social position or class distinctions, and in fact as society becomes complex, items of decorative clothing or adornment become distinctive of rank and position.

Georg Simmel (1904), in his classic discussion of fashion change, points out that fashion is a process of imitation, not evolution. In the process of fashion change, emulation leads to imitation, and imitation leads to both equalization and the need for further differentiation. Unlike Spencer (1896) and Darwin (1872), where change in forms of dress is an evolving linear progression, Simmel proposes that change in fashion is cyclic. Innovation in fashion originates in the elite social classes and fashion differentiates not only one era from another but also one social class from those below it. This idea forms the basis for the trickle-down theory of fashion change. Simmel claims that the process of fashion change requires a differentiated society. Fashion is a form of class differentiation and is a recurrent natural process of change.

Elizabeth Hurlock (1929), in an essay based on her dissertation, tests prevalent theories and explanations concerning motives for fashion change and clothing selection. These theories include Spencer's (1896) ideas about fashion as evolution and Simmel's (1904) trickle-down theory among others. She based her questionnaire on suggestions listed in the work of Hall (1898), Flaccus (1906), and Rusling (1905), and from the "many theories regarding the motives at the basis of fashion, and from suggestions made by a group of graduate students at Columbia University" (p. 38). She gathered data from a total of 1,452 individuals who were students in high school or college settings, both males and females, with ages ranging from 16 to 51. She analyzed the responses of these individuals to determine which theories and which motives were refuted or supported by contemporaneous behavior. In her tests of these theories and explanations, her results do not support that changes in fashion result from imitation and differentiation or as a result of a desire for attraction. Rather, she finds that the desire for novelty is a predominant reason for fashion change.

Edward Sapir (1931) writes a definition of the concept of fashion for the *Encyclopedia of the Social Science* from an anthropological perspective. In this excerpt, Sapir clarifies the concept of fashion and compares it to other related concepts such as fad, classic, or custom. For Sapir, "fashion is custom in the guise of departure from custom" (p. 140). He offers an explanation for fashion change as well as for gender differences in dress. Sapir says that fashion is an objective term that depends on context to give it its "emotional qualities" (p. 139). He critiques fashion and examines fashion as a symbol of the ego. In the excerpt we selected, his focus is on discussing the "fundamental drives leading to the creation and acceptance of fashion" (p. 140).

James Laver (1937) proposes a theory of fashion change by critiquing existing explanations for what he calls the origins of clothing. This work was written several years before it was published. In this excerpt Laver contends that "fashion begins with the discovery . . . that clothes could be used as a compromise between exhibitionism and modesty" (p. 200). Fashion change is not arbitrary, but can be explained by Flügel's (1930) theory of shifting erogenous zones, in which new styles of clothing reveal parts of the female body that were previously concealed. Laver contends that the sexuality of the female body makes for seductiveness, and in fact, this seductiveness drives fashion change. His explanation privileges the male gaze as women are eroticized in the juxtaposition between the shifting zones. The constant process of revealing and concealing aspects of a woman's body creates the explanation for a style's acceptance, but Laver is not as clear about why styles fall out of acceptance. According to Laver, writing in the 1930s, fashion change was accelerated by mass production within a class-based society. Laver echoes Simmel's (1904) earlier contention that fashion change is based on imitation and class differentiation. He also sees fashion as impacting multiple aspects of life, foreshadowing Blumer's (1939) analysis.

Predicting Fashion Change

Also addressing the topic of fashion change is Agnes Brooks Young (1937). Taking an evolutionary perspective, she strives to explain why fashion changes, how the changes take place, and shares how fashion can be predicted. Modeling her work after a method and analysis outlined by Kroeber (1919), she proposes principles in her explanation, the first that change is continuous; second, that change is slow; and third, that change is gradual. "Fashion change in women's dress is a continuous, slow process of modification" (p. 206). Her study of what she called "annual typicals" was based on analyzing over 8,000 fashion plates and magazine images that represented, in her view, the modal styles dating from 1760 to 1937. Her statistical analysis reveals three basic styles of women's skirt silhouettes – bell-shaped, back fullness, and tubular – that allow for the prediction of future fashion. She clearly tries to develop laws or principles to be tested and used to predict fashion change. Another component of her book is an explanation of why fashion changes. She presents logical reasons outlining the psychological benefits of change and emphasizes a phased cycle of change from an evolutionary perspective.

Fashion as Collective and Consumer Behavior

Herbert Blumer (1939) looks at fashion from a sociological perspective. He quickly points out that fashion is not narrowly limited to dress and has a much wider impact reaching into the fine arts as well as the hard sciences. Blumer echoes Simmel's (1904) and Laver's (1937) contention that fashion is based fundamentally on differentiation and emulation within a class-based society. Essentially, fashion is an important social movement with differing characteristics from other types of collective behavior. Fashion is "a genuine expressive movement" (p. 276), one based on subjective needs and one that supports and contributes to building shared experience and tastes.

Adam Smith (1759) approaches fashion from the perspective of economics. Our excerpt, drawn from one of the classics in the science of economics, presents his viewpoint that includes moral arguments and judgments. He discusses fashion as reserved for the upper social classes. He precedes Blumer (1939) in stating that fashion as change is not restricted to clothing styles or furniture but includes and impacts other aspects of the arts – literature, music, and architecture. Custom and fashion dominate judgments concerning the ideals of beauty. Ideals are what he calls "species-specific" (p. 288). Most interesting is his comment that what makes a member of each species beautiful is the most customary or average form rather than the unique form. Smith sees fashion as influencing notions of beauty, resulting in his making a moral judgement against being fashionable.

Thorstein Veblen (1894, 1899) also takes an economic approach to fashion as an important aspect of consumer behavior. He explains how dress became more than just a way to make an individual attractive to becoming a means of economic expression. In the debate on the motives for dressing the body, Veblen accepts the principle of adornment as a primary fact of social evolution. The motive behind dressing the body has evolved from an aesthetic expression to an economic one. What makes it an economic expression is that dress functions as an "index of the wealth of its wearer or, to be more precise, of its owner, for the wearer and owner are not necessarily the same person" (p. 199). Writing at the turn of the twentieth century, Veblen notes that the function of dress varies between men and women. Men's dress reflects utility whereas women's dress has come to symbolize her role as a "pecuniary possession" of her husband or father. In this aspect, women's dress is a means to display the earning and purchasing power of men. In Veblen's view, being fashionable becomes a moral concern, for he calls it not only wasteful expenditure but also wasteful consumption.

Estelle De Young Barr's (1934) excerpt, published from her dissertation, attempts scientifically to uncover the motives underlying an individual's choice of dress. Her approach is theoretical and takes into account a consumer point of view, not an economic one. She recognizes that choosing dress is a major social activity that serves as a medium for communication. In order to use dress as an effective communication medium, a person needs knowledge of design elements as well as knowledge of the self. As a result of her research findings, Barr discusses the important factors underlying consumer choice concerning dress, noting that there are multiple factors motivating an individual's choice. Choice is not reduced to just an economic or a communicative function; rather, the dress of an individual reflects a wider range of aesthetic, psychological, and practical considerations.

Reference

Flügel, J. C. (1932). *The psychology of clothes*. London: Hogarth Press.

Rusling, L.A. (1905). Children's attitudes toward clothes. *Pedagogical Seminary*, 12, 525–526.

6

Fashion as Change

Development in Dress *George H. Darwin*

The development of dress presents a strong analogy to that of organisms, as explained by the modern theories of evolution; and in this article I propose to illustrate some of the features which they have in common. We shall see that the truth expressed by the proverb, "Natura non facit saltum",[1] is applicable in the one case as in the other; the law of progress holds good in dress, and forms blend into one another with almost complete continuity. In both cases a form yields to a succeeding form, which is better adapted to the then surrounding conditions; thus, when it ceased to be requisite that men in active life should be ready to ride at any moment, and when riding had for some time ceased to be the ordinary method of travelling, knee breeches and boots yielded to trousers. The "Ulster Coat," now so much in vogue, is evidently largely fostered by railway travelling, and could hardly have flourished in the last century, when men either rode or travelled in coaches, where there was no spare room for any very bulky garment.

A new invention bears a kind of analogy to a new variation in animals; there are many such inventions, and many such variations; those that are not really beneficial die away, and those that are really good become incorporated by "natural selection," as a new item in our system. I may illustrate this by pointing out how macintosh-coats and crush-hats have become somewhat important items in our dress.

. . . But besides the general adaptation of dress above referred to, there is another influence which has perhaps a still more important bearing on the development of dress, and that is fashion. The love of novelty, and the extraordinary tendency which men have to exaggerate any peculiarity, for the time being considered a mark of good station in life, or handsome in itself, give rise I suppose to fashion. This influence bears no distant analogy to the "sexual selection," on which so much stress has recently been laid in the

1. Editor's note: *Natura non facit saltum* is translated as "Nature does not make a leap." Used frequently by Charles Darwin in his book *On the Origin of Species* (1859), the adage is originally attributed to Linnaeus and expresses the evolutionary ideas of gradual change and continuity.

"Descent of Man." Both in animals and dress, remnants of former stages of development survive to a later age, and thus preserve a tattered record of the history of their evolution.

These remnants may be observed in two different stages or forms. 1st. Some parts of the dress have been fostered and exaggerated by the selection of fashion, and are then retained and crystallized as it were, as part of our dress, notwithstanding that their use is entirely gone (*e.g.*, the embroidered pocket-flaps in a court uniform, now sewn fast to the coat). 2ndly. Parts originally useful have ceased to be of any service, and have been handed down in an atrophied condition . . .

COATS. – Everyone must have noticed the nick in the folded collar of the coat and the waistcoat; this is of course made to allow for the buttoning round the neck, but it is in the condition of a rudimentary organ, for the nick would probably not come in the right place, and in the waistcoat at least there are usually neither requisite buttons nor buttonholes . . .

. . . At the end of the seventeenth, and at the beginning of the eighteenth centuries, coats seem very commonly to have been furnished with slits running from the edge of the skirt, up under the arms, and these were made to button up, in a manner similar in all respects to the slit of the tails. The sword was usually worn under the coat, and the sword-hilt came through the slit on the left side. Later on these slits appear to have been sewed up, and the buttons and button-holes died away, with the exception of two or three buttons just at the top of the slits; thus in coats of about the year 1705, it is not uncommon to see several buttons clustered about the tops of all three slits. The buttons at the top of the centre slit entirely disappeared, but the two buttons now on the backs of our coats trace their pedigree up to those on the hips. Thus it is not improbable that although our present buttons represent those used for making the waist, as above explained, yet that they in part represent the buttons for fastening up these side slits.

. . . It was not until the reign of George III that coats were cut back at the waist, as are our present evening coats, but since, before that fashion was introduced, the coats had become swallowtailed in the manner explained, it seems likely that this form of coat, was suggested by the previous fashion. And, indeed, stages of development of a somewhat immediate character may be observed in old engravings. In the uniforms of the last century the coats were double-breasted, but were generally worn open, with the flaps thrown back and buttoned to rows of buttons on the coat. These flaps, of course, showed linings of the coat, and were of the same colour as the tails; the button-holes were usually embroidered, and thus the whole of the front of the coat became richly laced. Towards the end of the century the coats were made tight, and were fastened together in front by hooks, but the vestiges of the flaps remained in a double line of buttons, and in the front of the coat being of a different colour from that of the rest, and being richly laced. A uniform of this nature is still retained in some foreign armies. This seems also to explain the use of the term "facings" as applied to the collar and cuffs of a uniform, since, we shall see hereafter, they would be of the same colour as these flaps. It may also explain the habit of braiding the front of a coat, as is done in our Hussar and other regiments.

. . . I have now gone through the principle articles of men's clothing, and have shown how numerous and curious are the rudiments or "survivals," as Mr. Tylor calls them; a more thorough search proves the existence of many more. For instance, the various gowns worn at the Universities and elsewhere, afford examples. These gowns were, as late as the reign of Queen Elizabeth, simply upper garments,[2] but have survived into this age as mere badges. Their chief peculiarities consist in the sleeves, and it is curious that nearly all of such peculiarities point to various devices by which the wearing of sleeves has been eluded or rendered less burdensome. Thus the plaits and buttons in a barrister's gown, and the slit in front of the sleeve of the B.A.'s gown, are for this purpose. In an M.A.'s gown the sleeves extend below the knees, but there is a hole in the side through which the arm is passed; the end of the sleeve is sewed up, but there is a kind of scallop at the lower part, which represents the narrowing of the wrist. A barrister's gown has a small hood sewed to the left shoulder, which would hardly go on the head of an infant, even if it could be opened out into a hood shape.

It is not, however, in our dress alone that these survivals exist; they are to be found in all the things of our every-day life . . .

. . . It seems a general rule that on solemn or ceremonial occasions men retain archaic forms; thus it is that court dress survival of the every-day dress of the last century; that uniforms in general are richer in rudiments than common dress; that a carriage with a position is *de rigueur* at a wedding; and that (as mentioned by Sir John Lubbock) the priest of a savage nation, acquainted with the use of metals, still use a stone knife for their sacrifices – just as Anglican priests still prefer candles to gas.

The details given in this article, although merely curious, and perhaps insignificant in themselves, show that the study of dress from an evolutional standpoint serves as yet one further illustration of the almost infinite ramifications to which natural selection and its associated doctrines of development may be applied.

Source Excerpted from Darwin, G.H. (1872). Development in dress. *MacMillan's Magazine*, 410–416.

2. See figures, pp. 254, 311, Fairholt (1846).

Biographical note   Sir George Darwin (1845–1912) was the son of Charles Darwin. He was an English astronomer and professor at Cambridge University. He studied tidal effects on the planets, and tried unsuccessfully to apply evolutionary theory to explain the development of the moon. He was the first to apply mathematical techniques to study the evolution of the Sun-Earth-Moon system.

References

Darwin, Charles. (1961). *The origin of species* (The Harvard classics series, Vol. 11). New York: Collier.
Fairholt, F.W. (1846). *Costume in England*. London.

❖ ❖ ❖

Badges and Costumes *Herbert Spencer*

The pursuit of interpretations once more takes us back to victories achieved over men or animals. Badges are derived from trophies; with which, in early stages, they are identical. We have seen that by the Shoshones, a warrior is allowed to wear the feet and claws of a grizzly bear, constituting their "highest insignia of glory," only when he has killed one: the trophy being thus made into a recognized mark of honor. And seeing this, we cannot doubt that the buffalo-horns decorating the head of a Mandan chief and indicating his dignity, were at first worn as spoils of the chase in which he prided himself: implying a genesis of a badge out of a trophy, which gives meaning to the head-dresses of certain divine and human personages among ancient peoples. Beginning as a personal distinction naturally resulting from personal prowess, like the lion's skin which Hercules wears, the trophy-badge borne by a warrior whose superiority gains for him supremacy, tends to originate a family-badge; which becomes a badge of office if his descendants retain power. Hence the naturalness of the facts that in Ukimi "the skin [of a lion] . . . is prepared for the sultan's wear, as no one else dare use it;" that "a leopard-skin mantle is the insignia of rank among the Zoolus;" and that in Uganda, certain of the king's attendants wear "leopard-cat skins girt round the waist, the sign of royal blood."

Of course if skins or other parts of slain beasts, tend thus to become badges, so, too, do parts of slain men. "The Chichimecs flea their heads [of their vanquished enemies] and fit that skin upon their own heads with all the hair, and so wear it as a token of valour, till it rots off in bits." Here the scalp which proves his victory, is itself used in stamping the warrior as honorable.

Similarly when, of the Yucantanese, Landa says that "after a victory they tore from the slain enemy the jaw-bone, and having stripped it of flesh, they put it on their arm" we may recognize the beginning of another kind of badge from another kind of trophy. Though clear evidence that jawbones become badges, is not forthcoming, we have good reason to think that substituted representations of them do. After our war with Ashantee, where, as we have seen, jawbones are habitually taken as trophies, there were brought over to England among other curiosities, small models of jawbones made in gold, used for personal adornment. And facts presently to be cited suggest that they became ornaments after having originally been badges worn by those who had actually taken jawbones from enemies . . .

. . . Civilized usages obscure the truth that men were not originally prompted to clothe themselves by either the desire for warmth or the thought of decency . . . We are shown that the dress, like the badge, is at first worn from the wish for admiration.

Some of the facts already given concerning American Indians, who wear as marks of honour the skins of formidable animals they have killed, suggest that the badge and the dress have a common root, and that the dress is, at any rate in some cases, a collateral development of the badge . . . Whence it is inferable that the honourableness of the badge and of the dress, simultaneously arise from the honourableness of the trophy. That possession of a skin-dress passes into a class-distinction I find no direct proof; though, as the skins of formidable beasts often become distinctive of chiefs, it seems probable that skins in general become distinctive of a dominant class where a servile class exists. Indeed, in a primitive society there unavoidably arises this contrast between those who, engaged in the chase when not engaged in war, can obtain skin-garments, and those who, as slaves, are debarred from doing so by their occupation. Hence, possibly, the interdicts in medieval Europe against the wearing of furs by the inferior classes.

Even apart from this it is inferable that since, by taking his clothes, nakedness is commonly made a trait of the prisoner, and consequently of the slave, relative amount of clothing becomes a class-distinction. In some cases there result exaggerations of the difference thus incidentally arising. Where the inferior are clothed, the superior distinguish themselves by being more clothed . . .

. . . Of course with that development of ceremonial control which goes along with elaboration of political structure, differences of quantity, quality, shape and colour are united to produce dresses distinctive of classes. This trait is most marked where the rule is most despotic; as in China where "between the highest mandarin or prime minister and the lowest constable, there are nine classes, each distinguished by a dress peculiar to itself;" as in

Japan, where the attendants of the Mikado "are clad after a particular fashion
. . . and there is so much difference even among themselves, as to their habits,
that thereby alone it is easily known what rank they are of, or what employment they have at Court;" and as in European countries during times of
unchecked personal government, when each class had its distinctive costume.

The causes which have originated, developed, and specialized badges and
dresses, have done the like with ornaments; which have, indeed, the same
origins.

How trophy-badges pass into ornaments, we shall see on joining with facts
given at the outset of the chapter, certain kindred facts. In Guatemala, when
commemorating by war-dances the victories of earlier times, the Indians were
"dressed in the skins and wearing the heads of animals on their own;" and
among the Chibchas, persons of rank "wore helmets, generally made of the
skins of fierce animals." If we recall the statement already quoted, that in
primitive European times, the warrior's head and shoulders were protected
by the hide of a wild animal (the skin of its head sometimes surmounting his
head); and if we add the statement of Plutarch that the Cimbri wore helmets
representing the heads of wild beasts; we may infer that the animal-ornaments
on metal-helmets began as imitations of hunter's trophies. This inference is
supported by evidence already cited in part, but in part reserved for the present
occasion. The Ashantees who, as we have seen, take human jaws as trophies,
use both actual jaws and golden models of jaws for different decorative purposes: adorning their musical instruments, &c., with the realities, and carrying
on their persons the metallic representations. A parallel derivation occurs
among the Malagasy. When we read that by them silver ornaments like croc-
odile's teeth are worn on various parts of the body, we can scarcely doubt
that the silver teeth are substitutes for actual teeth originally worn as trophies.

We shall the less doubt this derivation on observing in how many parts of
the world personal ornaments are made out of these small and durable parts
of conquered men and animals – how by Caribs, Tupis, Moxos, Ashantees,
human teeth are made into armlets, anklets, and necklaces; and how in other
cases the teeth of beasts, mostly formidable, are used in like ways. The necklaces of the Land Dyaks contain tiger-cat's teeth; the New Guinea people
ornament their necks, arms, and waists with hogs' teeth; while the Sandwich
Islanders have bracelets of the polished tusks of the hog, with anklets of
dogs' teeth. Some Dacotahs wear "a kind of necklace of white bear's claws
three inches long." Among the Kukis "a common armlet worn by the men
consists of two semi-circular boar's tusks tied together so as to form a ring."
Enumerating objects hanging from a Dyah's ear, Boyle includes "two boar's
tusks, one alligator's tooth." And picturing what her life would be at home,
a captive New Zealand girl in her lament says – " the shark's tooth would

hang from my ear." Though small objects which are attractive in colour and shape, will naturally be used by the savage for decorative purposes, yet pride in displaying proofs of his prowess, will inevitably make him utilize fit trophies in preference to other things, when he has them. The motive which made Mandans have their buffalo-robes "fringed on one side with scalp-locks," which prompts a Naga chief to adorn the collar round his neck with "tufts of the hair of the persons he had killed" and which leads the Hottentots to ornament their heads with the bladders of the wild beasts they have slain, as Kolben tells us, will inevitably tend to transform trophies into decorations wherever it is possible. Indeed while I write I find direct proof that this is so . . .

And then from cases in which the ornament is an actual trophy or representation of a trophy, we pass to cases in which it avowedly stands in place of a trophy. Describing practices of the Chibchas, Acosta says that certain of their strongest and bravest men had "their lips, noses, and ears pierced, and from them hung strings of gold quills, the number of which corresponded with that of the enemies they had killed in battle:" the probability being that these golden ornaments, originally representations of actual trophies, had lost resemblance to them.

Thus originating, adornments of these kinds become distinctive of the warrior-class; and there result interdicts on the use of them by inferiors. Such interdicts have occurred in various places. Among the Chibchas, "paintings, decorations and jewels on dresses, and ornaments, were forbidden to the common people." So, too, in Peru, "none of the common people could use gold or silver except by special privilege." And without multiplying evidence from nearer regions, it will suffice to add that in medieval France, jewellery and plate were marks of distinction not allowed to those below a certain rank.

Of course decorations beginning as actual trophies, passing into representations of trophies made of precious materials, and, while losing their resemblance to trophies, coming to be marks of honour given to brave warriors by their militant rulers (as in Imperial Rome, where armlets were thus awarded) inevitably pass from relative uniformity to relative multiformity. As society complicates there result orders of many kinds – stars, crosses, medals, and the like. These it is observable are most if not all of them of military origin. And then where a militant organization evolved into rigidity, continues after the life has ceased to be militant, we find such decorations used to mark ranks of another kind; as in China, with its differently-coloured buttons distinguishing its different grades of mandarins.

I must not, however, be supposed to imply that this explanation covers all cases. Already I have admitted that the rudimentary aesthetic sense which leads the savage to paint his body, has doubtless a share in prompting the use of attractive objects for ornaments; and two other origins of ornaments must be added. Cook tells us that the New Zealanders carry suspended to their ears the nails and teeth of their deceased relations; and much more bulky relics, which are carried about by widows and others among some races, may also occasionally be modified into decorative objects. Further, it seems that badges of slavery undergo a kindred transformation. The ring through the nose, which Assyrian sculptures show us was used for leading captives taken in war, which marked those who, as priests, entered the service of certain gods in ancient America, and which in Astrachan is even now a sign of dedication, that is of subjection; seems elsewhere to have lost its meaning, and to have survived as an ornament. And this is a change analogous to that which has occurred with marks on the skin.

. . . How this diffusion of dresses marking honourable position and disuse of dresses marking inferiority, has gone far among ourselves, but is still incomplete, is shown in almost every household. On the one hand we have the fashionable gowns of cooks and housemaids; on the other hand we have that dwarfed representative of the muslin cap, which, once hiding the hair, was insisted upon by mistresses as a class distinction, but which, gradually dwindling, has now become a small patch on the back of the head: a good instance of the unobtrusive modifications by which usages are changed . . .

Source Excerpted from Spencer, H. (1924). *The principles of sociology*. New York and London: Appleton. (Original work published 1896)

Biographical note Herbert Spencer (1820–1903) was an English sociologist and philosopher of biological and social evolution. Although he received no formal training, his education was the result of his own extensive reading in the natural sciences. During his own time, Spencer was criticized by the academic establishment. Spencer studied human society from an evolutionary viewpoint, and is important as one of the first to establish the scientific study of human society. He is thought to have coined the phrase "survival of the fittest."

* * *

Fashion *Georg Simmel*

. . . Fashion is the imitation of a given example and satisfies the demand for social adaptation; it leads the individual upon the road which all travel, it furnishes a general condition, which resolves the conduct of every individual into a mere example. At the same time it satisfies in no less degree the need of differentiation, the tendency towards dissimilarity, the desire for change and contrast, on the one hand by a constant change of contents, which gives to the fashion of today an individual stamp as opposed to that of yesterday and of to-morrow, on the other hand because fashions differ for different classes – the fashions of the upper stratum of society are never identical with those of the lower; in fact, they are abandoned by the former as soon as the latter prepares to appropriate them. Thus fashion represents nothing more than one of the many forms of life by the aid of which we seek to combine in uniform spheres of activity the tendency towards social equalization with the desire for individual differentiation and change. Every phase of the conflicting pair strives visibly beyond the degree of satisfaction that any fashion offers to an absolute control of the sphere of life in question. If we should study the history of fashions (which hitherto have been examined only from the view-point of the development of their contents) in connection with their importance for the form of the social process, we should find that it reflects the history of the attempts to adjust the satisfaction of the two counter-tendencies more and more perfectly to the condition of the existing individual and social culture. The various psychological elements in fashion all conform to this fundamental principle.

Fashion, as noted above, is a product of class distinction and operates like a number of other forms, honor especially, the double function of which consists in revolving within a given circle and at the same time emphasizing it as separate from others. Just as the frame of a picture characterizes the work of art inwardly as a coherent, homogeneous, independent entity and at the same time outwardly severs all direct relations with the surrounding space, just as the uniform energy of such forms cannot be expressed unless we determine the double effect, both inward and outward, so honor owes its character, and above all its moral rights, to the fact that the individual in his personal honor at the same time represents and maintains that of his social circle and his class. These moral rights, however, are frequently considered unjust by those without the pale. Thus fashion on the one hand signifies union with those in the same class, the uniformity of a circle characterized by it, and, *uno actu*, the exclusion of all other groups.

Union and segregation are the two fundamental functions which are here inseparably united, and one of which, although or because it forms a logical contrast to the other, becomes the condition of its realization. Fashion is merely a product of social demands, even though the individual object which it creates or recreates may represent a more or less individual need. This is clearly proved by the fact that very frequently not the slightest reason can be found for the creations of fashion from the standpoint of an objective, aesthetic, or other expediency. While in general our wearing apparel is really adapted to our needs, there is not a trace of expediency in the method by which fashion dictates, for example, whether wide or narrow trousers, colored or black scarfs shall be worn. As a rule the material justification for an action coincides with its general adoption, but in the case of fashion there is a complete separation of the two elements, and there remains for the individual only this general acceptance as the deciding motive to appropriate it. Judging from the ugly and repugnant things that are sometimes in vogue, it would seem as though fashion were desirous of exhibiting its power by getting us to adopt the most atrocious things for its sake alone. The absolute indifference of fashion to the material standards of life is well illustrated by the way in which it recommends something appropriate in one instance, something abstruse in another, and something materially and aesthetically quite indifferent in a third. The only motivations with which fashion is concerned are formal social ones. The reason why even aesthetically impossible styles seem *distingué,* elegant, and artistically tolerable when affected by persons who carry them to the extreme, is that the persons who do this are generally the most elegant and pay the greatest attention to their personal appearance, so that under any circumstances we would get the impression of something *distingué* and aesthetically cultivated. This impression we credit to the questionable element of fashion, the latter appealing to our consciousness as the new and consequently most conspicuous feature of the *tout ensemble.*

Fashion occasionally will accept objectively determined subjects such as religious faith, scientific interests, even socialism and individualism; but it does not become operative as fashion until these subjects can be considered independent of the deeper human motives from which they have risen. For this reason the rule of fashion becomes in such fields unendurable. We therefore see that there is good reason why externals – clothing, social conduct, amusements – constitute the specific field of fashion, for here no dependence is placed on really vital motives of human action. It is the field which we can most easily relinquish to the bent towards imitation, which it would be a sin to follow in important questions. We encounter here a close connection between the consciousness of personality and that of the material forms of life, a connection that runs all through history. The more objective our view of life has become in the last centuries, the more it has stripped the picture of nature of all subjective and anthropomorphic elements, and the more sharply has the conception of individual personality become defined. The social regulation of our inner and outer life is a sort of embryo condition, in which the contrasts of the purely personal and the purely objective are differentiated, the action being synchronous and reciprocal. Therefore wherever man appears essentially as a social being we observe neither strict objectivity in the view of life nor absorption and independence in the consciousness of personality.

Social forms, apparel, aesthetic judgment, the whole style of human expression, are constantly transformed by fashion, in such a way, however, that fashion – *i.e.*, the latest fashion – in all these things affects only the upper classes. Just as soon as the lower classes begin to copy their style, thereby crossing the line of demarcation the upper classes have drawn and destroying the uniformity of their coherence, the upper classes turn away from this style and adopt a new one, which in its turn differentiates them from the masses; and thus the game goes merrily on. Naturally the lower classes look and strive towards the upper, and they encounter the least resistance in those fields which are subject to the whims of fashion; for it is here that mere external imitation is most readily applied. The same process is at work as between the different sets within the upper classes, although it is not always as visible here as it is, for example, between mistress and maid. Indeed, we may often observe that the more nearly one set has approached another, the more frantic becomes the desire for imitation from below and the seeking for the new from above. The increase of wealth is bound to hasten the process considerably and render it visible, because the objects of fashion, embracing as they do the externals of life, are most accessible to the mere call of money, and conformity to the higher set is more easily acquired here than in fields which demand an individual test that gold and silver cannot affect.

Source Excerpted from Simmel, G. (1904). Fashion. *International Quarterly, 10*, 130–155.

Biographical note Georg Simmel (1858–1918) was a German philosopher and sociologist. He established sociology as a field of study and made important contributions to sociological methodology. He is important to the field of apparel and textiles because he sought to specifically analyze and address the process of fashion. His most important contribution is his conception of sociology as an independent discipline.

✳ ✳ ✳

Motivation in Fashion *Elizabeth Hurlock*

. . . Few attempts have been made to determine the fundamental motives at the basis of fashions in clothing, or the motives involved in the selection of one type of clothing rather than another. Perhaps the difficulty of the problem itself is responsible for this lack of information. The study of human motives is always a difficult one, and this becomes increasingly so when personal motives are closely bound up with custom and tradition. There are many speculations and theories as to the why and wherefore of clothing, but it usually ends there. Historians and artists have recorded clothing fashions of the past, but what the motives were that inspired these fashions have either been ignored or passed over with a casual comment. Recently, philosophers, psychologists, economists, and designers have turned their attention to this phase of fashion analysis, and, as a result, we have the beginning of a scientific approach to the whole problem of clothing.

. . . The questionnaire used in this study was based on suggestions from the works of Hall, Flaccus and Rusling, from the many theories regarding the motives at the basis of fashion, and from suggestions made by a group of graduate students . . .

. . . The questionnaires were sent out from 1923 to 1928 and during this time one thousand, four hundred and fifty-two people recorded their opinions about fashion on these.

. . . In any experimental study, one of the most interesting as well as most important phases, is a direct comparison of its results with those of former studies. When, however, few studies have been made along the same general lines, and when there are many theoretical analyses, comparisons become especially interesting. The writer has therefore made an effort to compare the present work from every possible angle with previous studies along the same general lines. These comparisons will be subdivided into two groups, those that relate to theoretical studies, and those that relate to experimental studies. In the comparisons with the theoretical studies, analyses of motives, fashion changes and fashion's relation to sex, are taken up separately.

While Ross, Gault, Bogardus, Allport, Nystrom and other writers all hold that two ruling principles are at the basis of fashion, namely, Imitation and Differentiation, answers to this questionnaire did not agree with these principles. Seventy-seven per cent of the entire group used for the experiment said they did not follow fashions so as to appear equal to those having a higher social position than they, while only 23% admitted that they were ruled by this motive.

The desire to attract attention, or "self-advertisement," as it was described by Gault, Bernard and Allport, did not prove to be so powerful as believed by these authors. Only 17% of the group said they selected their clothing to draw attention to themselves and of this number 8% were men and 27% were women. A desire to combine becomingness with the prevailing style motivated 91% of the group, while 95% said they tried to make their clothing the background, rather than the outstanding feature of their personalities. In selecting colors, becomingness and utility ranked as prime motives in the majority of cases. Hence, it would seem that dress for the purpose of self-advertisement is not so commonly used as has been thought.

Dress as a means of compensation for physical or personality deficiencies, as suggested by Bernard, Allport and Nystrom, was used by 54% of the groups.

It is interesting to note that 72% of the women, as opposed to 38% of the men, said they used dress for this purpose. Eighty-eight per cent of the group, of which 95% were women and 82% men, said they selected their clothing with the idea of bringing out their best qualities. It would seem, therefore, that the compensatory value of clothing is very great, and theory here is substantiated by fact.

The rôle of fear in fashion, which has been so greatly stressed by Dearborn is justified by the results of this study. One-hundred per cent of the men and 86% of the women, making a combined average of 93%, claimed that they preferred to have a style well established before adopting it. Dearborn's "clothes-fear," it would seem, is responsible for this conservatism.

The use of clothes for economic display, which has been so strongly emphasized by Veblen, does not stand out as conscious motive, though indirectly the members of the group used for the study show that they were dominated by it. Seventy-four per cent said they did not always try to dress so as to appear prosperous; while 55% only said they would be willing to deprive themselves of certain pleasures in order to be in style. When asked if they would be willing to deprive themselves of certain necessities in order to be in style, the answer was negative in three-quarters of the cases. The use of dress as a means of creating the impression of being a person of leisure proved to be a conscious motive in the case of only 12% of the entire group. These results, therefore, are distinctly not in agreement with Veblen's theory or, perhaps it would be more accurate to say that the subjects used for this study were unconscious of being influenced by such motives.

Many theories have been given in answer to the question, why do fashions change? and these theories, like those in regard to fashion motives, are often very conflicting. The present analysis includes several questions which relate definitely to fashion changes, and, in view of the theories, the answers given in this study are very interesting. To 64% of the group, the desire for novelty, which was stressed by Nystrom as one of the most important factors in change, was given as their reason for changing styles from season to season. Only 12% said they do so to avoid the appearance of poverty, which to Veblen stands out as the most important single motive in fashion changes. Dearborn's "clothes-fear" seems to have been operative in one-quarter of the group who said they accepted fashion changes so as to avoid social criticism.

The relation of clothing to sex was analyzed in several of the questions. Thirty-eight per cent of the group, of which number, 41% were women and 36% men, said they dressed so as to win the approval of their own sex. Thorndike, it may be remembered states firmly that "women obviously dress for other women's eyes." While 25% of the group admitted that they dressed to please the opposite sex, 36% said they dressed to win the approval of both sexes. From these answers, it would seem that the desire to win approval as such is stronger than the sex motive so often attributed in popular literature to fashion.

The influence of modesty, which might be considered an out growth of the sex motive, is seen in the answers . . . Ninety per cent of the group, of which there was a slightly higher percentage of men than of women, said that they would refuse to accept certain prevailing styles because they thought them immodest. While many writers who have studied the possible causes underlying the origin of clothing, have stressed the modesty factor, it is interesting to note that writers of present-day fashion motivation have given little or no attention to this factor. And yet, from the large percentage of the group that stressed this point, it is obvious that modesty is an important motive in the acceptance or rejection of a fashion.

Comparisons with former experimental studies have brought to light some interesting data. The emphasis which Hall and Flaccus have laid on the effect of clothing upon children's behavior and happiness, has been corroborated by the present study, the subjects of which were of more mature years. In this study, 92% of the group said that dress affected their behavior and 95%, that it affected their happiness. Dearborn's emphasis on the relationship between clothing and efficiency was also confirmed. Eighty-eight per cent of the group, of which it is interesting to note that 94% were women and only 83% men, said that dress so affected their efficiency that they could do better work if they felt they were well dressed. Almost 100% of the women and 94% of the men said that their feeling of self-confidence was increased by being well and appropriately dressed,

Indirectly the relationship between clothing and success in life, which Dearborn emphasized so strongly, may be seen in the answers . . . One-hundred per cent of the men and 99% of the women claimed that their estimates of people were influenced by the effects their clothing made on them, while 80% said this held only for first impressions. Nevertheless, first impressions in the business and social world are often very important factors in determining success or failure. When asked if they spent a disproportionate amount of their incomes on clothes, 42% said "professional advancement" and 17%, a "good front" were the motivating causes. In as much as 33% claimed they did not spend disproportionate amounts, it is conclusive that those who do, do so because they believe that success and good appearance go hand in hand.

The Photoplay research study which laid great emphasis on the rôle of youth in present-day fashion matters, seems not to have exaggerated this rôle, so far as the results of this study may be taken as conclusive evidence. Ninety per cent of the group studied said they had noticed a change in their attitude toward clothing from childhood until the present time. In 67% of the cases, adolescence was the period in which clothes interest was strongest, while in 33%, it was during mature years.

Adolescence for two-thirds of the group and maturity for one-third, seem to be the times when social approval of one's clothing is most strong and influential in the individual's life.

Two-thirds of the group claimed that adolescence was the period of life in which happiness, efficiency and behavior were most affected by clothes, and one-third laid emphasis on maturity as the more important period. The same percentage claimed that their self-confidence was increased by being well-dressed in adolescence and maturity.

The rôle of reason or common sense has not been stressed either in the theoretical or experimental studies which have appeared before this study was made. Somehow or other, students of fashion motivation have ignored these motives, or have looked upon them as of lesser value than the motives they have emphasized, and hence have overlooked them. The present study, however, has shown that this is unjustified. Reason plays an important rôle in fashion motivation to-day, and it must be ranked with the other motives as powerful in determining the fashions of the hour. According to the answers given . . . 89% of the group, of which 95% consisted of men and 82% of women, said they always considered whether or not clothes would be useful to them when they made their selections. In 87% of the cases, the cost was always taken into consideration in the selection, and once again, this was true of a slightly larger percentage of the men than of the women. Disapproval of a prevailing fashion, because it would prove to be detrimental to health, or for some other good reason, would hold back 90% of the men and 79% of the women in adopting it. It is evident, therefore, that reason cannot justifiably be omitted from the list of fashion motives, and that fashion designers would do well to appeal strongly to this motive, especially when dealing with young people.

In summarizing the comparisons between this study and those previously made, it may be said that on the whole, the agreement is strong. The greatest amount of agreement, however, comes in the comparison with experimental studies, while many of the widely heralded theories seem to fall down under evidence of the sort brought forth in this study.

Source Excerpted from Hurlock, E.B. (1929). Motivation in fashion. *Archives of Psychology, 17*(3): 5–71.

Biographical note Elizabeth Hurlock (1898–1988) received her Ph.D. in psychology from Columbia University in 1924. She wrote many books on psychology on such topics as child development and adolescent development in addition to her work on fashion motivations. She taught at Columbia University and at University of Pennsylvania.

References

Allport, F. (1924). *Social psychology*. Cambridge, MA: Houghton Mifflin.

Bernard, L.I. (1926*). An introduction to social psychology*. New York: Henry Holt.

Bogardus, E.S. (1924). Social psychology of fads. *Journal of Applied Sociology*, 8, 239–243.

Dearborn, G. (1918). The psychology of clothing. *The Psychological Monographs*, 26, 1–72.

Flaccus, L.W. (1906). Remarks on the psychology of clothes. *Pedagogical Seminary*, 13, 61–83.

Gault, R. (1923). *Social psychology*. New York: Henry Holt.

Hall, G.S. (1897–1898). Early sense of self. *American Journal of Psychology*, 9, 351–395.

Nystrom, P. (1928*). Economics of fashion*. New York: Ronald Press.

Ross, E.A. (1917) *Social psychology*. New York: Macmillan.

Rusling, L.A. (1905.) Children's attitudes toward clothes. *Pedagogical Seminary*, 12, 525–526.

Thorndike, E. (1914). Educational psychology – Briefer course. New York: Columbia University.

Veblen, T. (1894). The economic theory of women's dress. *Popular Science Monthly*, 46, 198–205.

* * *

Fashion *Edward Sapir*

The fundamental drives leading to the creation and acceptance of fashion can be isolated. In the more sophisticated societies boredom, created by leisure and too highly specialized forms of activity, leads to restlessness and curiosity. This general desire to escape from the trammels of a too regularized existence is powerfully reinforced by a ceaseless desire to add to the attractiveness of the self and all other objects of love and friendship. It is precisely in functionally powerful societies that the individual's ego is constantly being convicted of helplessness. The individual tends to be unconsciously thrown back on himself and demands more and more novel affirmations of his effective reality. The endless rediscovery of the self in a series of petty truancies from the official socialized self becomes a mild obsession of the normal individual in any society in which the individual has ceased to be a measure of the society itself. There is, however, always the danger of too great a departure from the recognized symbols of the individual, because his identity is likely to be destroyed. That is why insensitive people, anxious to be literally in the fashion, so often overreach themselves and nullify the very purpose of fashion. Good hearted women of middle age generally fail in the art of being ravishing nymphs.

Somewhat different from the affirmation of the libidinal self is the more vulgar desire for prestige or notoriety, satisfied by changes in fashion. In this category belongs fashion as an outward emblem of personal distinction or of membership in some group to which distinction is ascribed. The imitation of fashion by people who belong to circles removed from those which set the fashion has the function of bridging the gap between a social class and the class next above it. The logical result of the acceptance of a fashion by all members of society is the disappearance of the kinds of satisfaction responsible for the change of fashion in the first place. A new fashion becomes psychologically necessary, and thus the cycle of fashion is endlessly repeated.

Fashion is emphatically a historical concept. A specific fashion is utterly unintelligible if lifted out of its place in a sequence of forms. It is exceedingly dangerous to rationalize or in any other way psychologize a particular fashion on the basis of general principles which might be considered applicable to the class of forms of which it seems to be an example. It is utterly vain, for instance, to explain particular forms of dress or types of cosmetics or methods of wearing the hair without a preliminary historical critique. Bare legs among modern women in summer do not psychologically or historically create at all the same fashion as bare legs and bare feet among primitives living in the tropics. The importance of understanding fashion historically should be obvious enough when it is recognized that the very essence of fashion is that it be valued as a variation in an understood sequence, as a departure from the immediately preceding mode.

Changes in fashion depend on the prevailing culture and on the social ideals which inform it. Under the apparently placid surface of culture there are always powerful psychological drifts of which fashion is quick to catch the direction. In a democratic society, for instance, if there is an unacknowledged drift toward class distinctions fashion will discover endless ways of giving it visible form. Criticism can always be met by the insincere defense that fashion is merely fashion and need not be taken seriously. If in a puritanic society there is a growing impatience with the outward forms of modesty, fashion finds it easy to minister to the demands of sex curiosity, while the old mores can be trusted to defend fashion with an affectation of unawareness of what fashion is driving at. A complete study of the history of fashion would undoubtedly throw much light on the ups and downs of sentiment and attitude at various periods of civilization. However, fashion never permanently outruns discretion and only those who are taken in by the superficial rationalizations of fashion are surprised by the frequent changes of face in its history. That there was destined to be a lengthening of women's skirts after they had become short enough was obvious from the outset to all except those who do not believe that sex symbolism is a real factor in human behavior.

The chief difficulty of understanding fashion in its apparent vagaries is the lack of exact knowledge of the unconscious symbolisms attaching to forms, colors, textures, postures and other expressive elements in a given culture. The difficulty is appreciably increased by the fact that the same expressive elements tend to have quite different symbolic references in different areas.

Source Excerpted from Sapir, E. (1931). Fashion. *Encyclopedia of the social sciences*. Vol 6. New York: Macmillan. Reprinted by permission from the Encyclopedia of the Social Sciences.

Biographical note Edward Sapir (1884–1939) is a foremost figure in American anthropological linguistics. An ethnolinguist, Sapir was a student of Franz Boas at Columbia University and is well known for his work on American Indian languages. He held appointments at Universities of California, Pennsylvania, and Chicago, then led the study of cultural anthropology at Yale University.

❖ ❖ ❖

Some Conclusions *James Laver*

The old fashioned moralist's view – a view not quite extinct among the upper clergy – was that fashion changed because women were incurably frivolous and inconstant. "*La donna è mobile . . .*"[1] But we have seen that fashion's changes are never entirely arbitrary: they always have some inner historical significance, so that the inadequacy of the female character cannot be a complete explanation. Women themselves generally see in fashion's changes an ever-progressing evolution towards something more sensible in the way of dress. Most women, if questioned on this point, will give as their opinion that the fashions of yesterday were indeed ridiculous, and that the fashions of the present day are both beautiful and practical. Women were probably always of this opinion, and all that can be said about it is that it is a complete delusion. Practicality plays a very minor part in the formation of fashion. If it were not so women would not have worn crinolines in the days when buses

1. Editor's note: "Woman is fickle" Translated from Italian: title of tenor aria from Verdi opera *Rigoletto*.

and railway carriages were at their very narrowest; nor would they to-day grope for brake and accelerator through the confusion of a trailing evening skirt. They would have adopted something like the fashion of 1927, and kept to it for ever. The psychologists have come forward with another explanation, that is probably very much nearer the truth, however unflattering it may be to the ears of emancipated women.

There are probably now very few among those who have studied the subject of clothes, either from the anthropological or the psychological angle, who hold that the origin of clothing is to be found in the impulse of modesty. It is generally agreed that the main impulse among primitive people comes, on the contrary, from the desire for display, such display consisting in its most primitive forms of a decorative emphasis on those very parts of the body which modesty leads us to hide. Protection, as a motive for clothing, is now relegated to a very minor *rôle*, and sometimes dismissed as a mere rationalization of a process which has other causes. Even those who still hold that clothing had its origin in modesty are as convinced as their opponents of the sexual significance of bodily coverings of all kind. But such sexual significance has, since men made the great renunciation at the end of the eighteenth century, been confined almost exclusively to female attire.[2] The sexuality of the female body is more diffused than that of the male, and as it is habitually covered up the exposure of any one part of it focuses the erotic attention, conscious or unconscious, and makes for seductiveness. Fashion really begins with the discovery in the fifteenth century that clothes could be used as a compromise between exhibitionism and modesty. The *dècolletage*, however, which arose at this period has been dealt with in another chapter. It is sufficient here to note that the aim of fashion ever since has been the exposure of, or the emphasis upon, the various portions of the female body taken in series.

The main fact which emerges from the experiences of nudists in modern times is that while the imaginative contemplation of the naked body may be a highly erotic proceeding, the actual experience is exactly the reverse. It is not a matter of beauty or ugliness, but simply that the eye becomes so accustomed to the naked human body that it ceases to have any meaning to the imagination at all. Since the relaxations of prudery during the last ten years even the costumes of the lighter stage have exhibited the same law; in fact, men have become so accustomed to seeing certain parts of the female body exposed that they no longer get any excitement out of the spectacle at all. In 1900 old gentlemen used to faint when they caught a passing glimpse of a

2. For a full discussion of these problems see Dr. J.C. Flügel's *Psychology of Clothes* (the International PsychoAnalystic Library, London, 1930).

female ankle. The modern young man can contemplate without emotion the entire area of the female leg and a considerable portion of the female stomach. In the nineteen-twenties, for the first time for many hundreds of years, the female leg was exposed to general view. The bust, however, also for the first time for many centuries, was not supposed to exist at all, and women who did not mind in the least exposing their lower limbs would have been embarrassed if called upon to wear a deep *dècolletage*.[3]

In short, the female body consists of a series of sterilized zones, which are those exposed by the fashion which is just going out, and an erogenous zone, which will be the point of interest for the fashion which is just coming in. This erogenous zone is always shifting, and it is the business of fashion to pursue it, without ever actually catching it up. It is obvious that if you really catch it up you are immediately arrested for indecent exposure. If you almost catch it up you are celebrated as a leader of fashion.

Granting, however, that this is an explanation of why fashions come in, it is not a complete explanation of why they go out, for in the eclipse of every fashion a large social – one might say snobbish – element is involved. The speeding up of fashion's changes during the last hundred years is due to several causes, chiefly to large-scale production and to the survival of snobbery into a democratic world.

The breakdown of the social hierarchy leaves every woman (for man has ceased to compete) free to dress as well as she can afford, with the result that the only possible superiority is the slight one of cut or material, or the short one of adopting a new fashion a little sooner than her neighbors. The latest creations of the great Paris *couturiers* are copied and duplicated almost as soon as they appear in the shops, so that the fashionable woman is forced to adopt something still newer in order to preserve her advantage. Fashion, in a word, filters steadily down in the social scale. The actual garments which express it become less and less adequate, owing to the use of poorer material and because they are less skilfully made. A fashion, therefore, very quickly becomes dowdy, and this is sufficient to induce women who can afford it to

---

3. During the rehearsals of Nymph Errant at the Adelphi Theatre in 1933 the practice dress of most of the chorus girls consisted of backless bathing costume. No one thought anything of this – least of all the girls themselves. But the day came for dress rehearsal, and in one of the scenes it was found that Doris Zinkeisen had devised for the chorus a costume very much like the male costume of 1830: tailcoat, trousers, waistcoat, etc. The front of the waistcoat, however, was cut low, so as to form a kind of *décolletage*. It was not a very startling *décolletage* – certainly no lower than would have been worn without any embarrassment by an *ingénue* of the eighties when attending her first ball. But there was a strike among the chorus against the indecency of this costume, and Mr. Cochran was compelled to fill up the offending gap with gauze.

change it as quickly as possible. After a while it becomes worse than dowdy: it becomes hideous, and this may be confirmed by the simple process of showing to any woman a photograph of the dress which she herself wore ten years before.

In fact, the following list might be established. The same costume will be:

Indecent	10 years before its time
Shameless	5 years before its time
Outré (daring)	1 year before its time
Smart	
Dowdy	1 year after its time
Hideous	10 years after its time
Ridiculous	20 years after its time
Amusing	30 years after its time
Quaint	50 years after its time
Charming	70 years after its time
Romantic	100 years after its time
Beautiful	150 years after its time

In the race for *chic* – that is, for contemporary seductiveness – which is the essence of fashion, certain members of the community get left behind. These are either older women, who have given up the struggle, or poor women, women so poor that they cannot afford to struggle at all. That some duchesses are ill dressed, and that some women who are well dressed have not a penny in the bank, does not affect the argument. Contrary to the expectations of Liberal reformers in the nineteenth-century, the more you abolish differences of caste and rank, the more desperate does the struggle for *chic* become, because it is only so that a woman can demonstrate superiority . . .

. . . The foregoing list shows quite clearly that there is no validity in our judgment concerning fashion until a certain period has elapsed: in short, there is a gap in appreciation; and it is the thesis of the present chapter that this gap in appreciation is not to be found only in questions of women's dress, but in every other matter of taste.

Source Excerpted from Laver, J. (1937). *Tastes and fashion: From the French revolution until today.* London: G.G. Harrap.

Biographical note James Laver (1899–1975) worked as keeper for 37 years in the department of engraving, illustration, and design at London's Victoria and Albert Museum. His interest in the history and psychology of costume began through his desire to date paintings by the costume depicted. He is best remembered for his theory of cycles of fashion, and the relationship between dress and the economic and social factors controlling the evolution of taste.

7

Predicting Fashion Change

On the Nature of Fashion *Agnes Brooks Young*

. . . The essence of fashion is change, and the chief value of the long series of annual typicals is that it provides a means for studying what it is that changes in fashion from year to year, and how the changes take place. This book attempts to answer those two questions. In the course of the study there have been developed certain general conclusions about the nature and processes of fashion change. Three of these general conclusions appear to be always valid.

The first of them is that fashion change in women's dress is always a continuous process. The typical fashion of each year always differs from that of the preceding year and that of the following year. There are no duplicates and no repetitions among the annual typicals.

The second general rule is that fashion change in women's dress is always a slow process. No annual typical differs in marked degree from its predecessor or from its successor. This is not in accord with the popular beliefs concerning fashion changes, which appear to hold that rates of change are highly variable, and that from time to time sweeping innovations appear. Probably these popular impressions have developed because waves of current interest in fashions are of widely varying intensity, and so give rise to the belief that fashion changes are sudden, capricious and unpredictable. This wide variability in the degree of public interest in women's fashions was well exemplified in the ferment of popular discussion concerning the short skirts of the middle 1920's.

The third principle is that fashion change in women's dress always proceeds by the modification of what has previously prevailed, and never by abrupt departure from it. Each new fashion can be traced back to its predecessor, for it is always an outgrowth or an adaptation in which the lineal descent is clearly evident.

These three general principles may be combined in the statement that fashion change in women's dress is a continuous, slow process of modification.

There are three other conclusions of a somewhat different character which are derived from the study of the long series of annual typicals illustrated in

Figure 2. Recurring examples of the back-fullness contour.

Figure 7.1a The three series of recurring "annual typicals" proposed by Young are based on the silhouette and shape of the woman's skirt. They are called the bell, the back-fullness, and the tubular. According to Young, these three skirt types have succeeded one another in that order of sequence in cycles lasting approximately thirty-three years. Figure 2 from *Recurring Cycles of Fashion, 1760–1937* (pp. 14–16), by A.B. Young, 1937, New York: Harper and Brothers. Reprinted with permission.

Figure 3. Recurring examples of the tubular contour.

Figure 7.1b Figure 3 from *Recurring Cycles of Fashion, 1760–1937* (pp. 14–16), by A.B. Young, 1937, New York: Harper and Brothers. Reprinted with permission.

Figure 4. Recurring examples of the bell-shaped contour.

Figure 7.1c Figure 4 from *Recurring Cycles of Fashion, 1760–1937* (pp. 14–16), by A.B. Young, 1937, New York: Harper and Brothers. Reprinted with permission.

this book. They may not be fundamental principles, for possibly the developments of future fashion changes may alter them by introducing exceptions from them. They are statements concerning the ways in which fashion changes have taken place during the past century and three-quarters.

The first of these general observations is that, as far back as these records run, changes in the fashion of women's dress have been grouped in well-defined cycles, during each of which the continuous evolution has consisted of modifications of a single type of dress characterized by the form and contour of its skirt.

The second of these three observations about the historic pattern of fashion behavior is that there have been so far only three of these accepted types of street dress skirts. These three types are the bell, the back-fullness and the tubular, and during the entire period covered by these records these three skirt types have succeeded one another in that unvarying order of sequence.

The third of these three significant general facts revealed by these records is that the succession of these three skirt types, and of the dress cycles consisting of modifications based on them, has so far taken place on an almost regular time schedule in which each cycle has lasted for approximately one-third of a century.

It may well prove that this curiously regular pattern of fashion evolution will be modified in the years to come. It is possible that a modification is under way even now, for this present dress cycle based on the tubular skirt has already lasted so long that, according to historic precedent, it has used up its allotted span of years. We cannot yet tell how this may prove to be, but we are warranted in believing that we shall be able to understand and interpret the developments, as time reveals them, only if we employ in our studies such measuring instruments as the scale of annual typicals presented here.

Source Excerpted from Young, A.B. (1937). *Recurring cycles of fashion.* New York: Harper and Brothers. Reprinted by permission from the publisher.

Biographical note Agnes Brooks Young (1898–1974) was an author and artist. She headed the costume department (1928–1929) at the Yale University Theater, and was lecturer on art and the psychology of dress at Western Reserve University (1930–1932). She authored twelve books on topics related to medicine, surgery, and the art and psychology of dress.

8

Fashion as Collective and Consumer Behavior

Fashion Movements *Herbert Blumer*

While fashion is thought of usually in relation to clothing, it is important to realize that it covers a much wider domain. It is to be found in manners, the arts, literature, and philosophy, and may even reach into certain areas of science. In fact, it may operate in any field of group life, apart from the technological and utilitarian area and the area of the sacred. Its operation requires a class society, for in its essential character it does not occur either in a homogenous society like a primitive group, nor in a caste society.

Fashion behaves as a movement, and on this basis it is different from custom which, by comparison, is static. This is due to the fact that fashion is based fundamentally on differentiation and emulation. In a class society, the upper classes or so-called social elite, are not able to differentiate themselves by *fixed* symbols or badges. Hence the more external features of their life and behavior are likely to be imitated by classes immediately subjacent to them, who, in turn, are initiated by groups immediately below them in the social structure. This process gives to fashion a vertical descent. However, the elite class finds that it is no longer distinguishable, by reason of the imitation made by others, and hence is led to adopt new differentiating criteria, only to displace these as they in turn are imitated. It is primarily this feature that makes fashion into a movement and which has led one writer to remark that a fashion, once launched, marches to its doom.

As a movement, fashion shows little resemblance to any of the other movements which we have considered. While it occurs spontaneously and moves along in a characteristic cycle, it involves little in the way of crowd behavior and it is not dependent upon the discussion process and the resulting public opinion. It does not depend upon the mechanisms of which we have spoken. The participants are not recruited through agitation or proselyting. No *esprit de corps* or morale is built up among them. Nor does the fashion movement have, or require, an ideology. Further, since it does not have a leadership imparting conscious direction to the movement, it does not build up a set of tactics. People participate in the fashion movement voluntarily and in response to the interesting and powerful kind of control which fashion imposes on them.

Not only is the fashion movement unique in terms of its character, but it differs from other movements in that it does not develop into a society. It does not build up a social organization; it has no personnel or functionaries; it does not develop a division of labor among its participants with each being assigned a given status; it does not construct a set of symbols, myths, values, philosophy, or set of practices, and in this sense does not form a culture; and finally, it does not develop a set of loyalties or form a we-consciousness.

Nevertheless, the movement of fashion is an important form of collective behavior with very significant results for the social order. First, it should be noted that the fashion movement is a genuine expressive movement. It does not have a conscious goal which people are trying to reach through collective action, as is true in the case of the specific social movements. Nor does it represent the release of excitement and tension generated in a dancing crowd situation. It is expressive, however, of certain fundamental impulses and tendencies, such as an inclination toward novel experience, a desire for distinction, and an urge to conform. Fashion is important especially in providing a means for the expression of developing tastes and disposition; this feature establishes it as a form of expressive behavior.

The latter remark provides a cue for understanding the rôle of fashion and the way in which it contributes to the formation of a new social order. In a changing society, such as is necessarily presupposed for the operation of fashion, people are continually having their subjective lives upset; they experience new dispositions and tastes which, however, are vague and ill-defined. It seems quite clear that fashion, by providing an opportunity for the expression of dispositions and tastes, serves to make them definite and to channelize them and, consequently, to fix and solidify them. To understand this, one should appreciate the fact that the movement and success of fashion are dependent upon the acceptance of the given style or pattern. In turn, this acceptance is based not merely upon the prestige attached to the style but also upon whether the style meets and answers to the dispositions and developing tastes of people. (The notorious failures that attend efforts to make styles fashionable upon the basis of mere prestige provide some support for this point.) From this point of view, we can regard fashion as arising and flourishing in response to new subjective demands. In providing means for the expression of these dispositions and tastes, fashion acts, as suggested before, to shape and crystallize these tastes. In the long run fashion aids, in this manner, to construct a *Zeitgeist* or a common subjective life, and in doing so, helps to lay the foundation for a new social order.

Source   Excerpted from Blumer, H. (1939). Fashion movements. In R.E. Park (Ed.), *An outline of the principles of sociology* (pp. 275–277). New York: Barnes and Noble.

Biographical note   Herbert Blumer (1900–1987) was an American sociologist. He studied under George Mead and received his doctorate from the University of Chicago in 1928. He taught at the University of Chicago from 1928 to 1951, and at University of California-Berkeley from 1952 until 1967 when he retired. Blumer is considered the father of symbolic interactionism. In 1983, he received the American Sociological Association's highest recognition, The Award for a Career of Distinguished Scholarship (*American National Biography*, vol. 3, pp 73–76).

* * *

Of the Influence of Custom and Fashion upon our Notions of Beauty and Deformity *Adam Smith*

. . . Fashion is different from custom, or rather is a particular species of it. That is not the fashion which every body wears, but which those wear who are of a high rank or character. The graceful, the easy, and commanding manners of the great, joined to the usual richness and magnificence of their dress, give a grace to the very form which they happen to bestow upon it. As long as they continue to use this form, it is connected in our imaginations with the idea of something that is genteel and magnificent, and though in itself it should be indifferent, it seems, on account of this relation, to have something about it that is genteel and magnificent too. As soon as they drop it, it loses all the grace which it had appeared to possess before, and being now used only by the inferior ranks of people, seems to have something of their meanness and awkwardness.

Dress and furniture are allowed by all the world to be entirely under the dominion of custom and fashion. The influence of those principles, however, is by no means confined to so narrow a sphere, but extends itself to whatever is in any respect the object of taste – to music, to poetry, to architecture. The modes of dress and furniture are continually changing; and that fashion appearing ridiculous to-day which was admired five years ago, we are experimentally convinced that it owed its vogue chiefly or entirely to custom and fashion. Clothes and furniture are not made of very durable materials. A well-fancied coat is done in a twelvemonth, and cannot continue longer to propagate, as the fashion, that form according to which it was made. The modes of furniture change less rapidly than those of dress; because furniture is commonly more durable. In five or six years, however, it generally undergoes an entire revolution, and every man in his own time sees the fashion in this respect change many different ways. The productions of the other arts are much more lasting, and, when happily imagined, may continue to propagate the fashion of their make for a much longer time. A well contrived building may endure many centuries; a beautiful air may be delivered down, by a sort of tradition, through many successive generations; a well-written poem may last as long as the world; and all of them continue for ages together to give the vogue to that particular style, to that particular taste or manner, according to which each of them was composed. Few men have an opportunity of seeing in their own times the fashion in any of these arts change very considerably. Few men have so much experience and acquaintance with the different modes which have obtained in remote ages and nations, as to be thoroughly reconciled to them, or to judge with impartiality between them and what takes place in their own age and country. Few men, therefore, are willing to allow, that custom or fashion have much influence upon their judgments concerning what is beautiful, or otherwise, in the productions of any of those arts; but imagine that all the rules which they think ought to be observed in each of them are founded upon reason and nature, not upon habit or prejudice. A very little attention, however, may convince them of the contrary, and satisfy them that the influence of custom and fashion over dress and furniture is not more absolute than over architecture, poetry, and music.

. . . Neither is it only over the productions of the arts that custom and fashion exert their dominion. They influence our judgments in the same manner with regard to the beauty of natural objects. What various and opposite forms are deemed beautiful in different species of things! The proportions which are admired in one animal are altogether different from those which are esteemed in another. Every class of things has its own peculiar conformation, which is approved of, and has a beauty of its own, distinct from that of every other species. It is upon this account that a learned Jesuit, Father Buffier, has determined that the beauty of every object consists in that form and colour, which is most usual among things of that particular sort to which it belongs. Thus in the human form the beauty of each feature lies in a certain middle, equally removed from a variety of other forms that are ugly. A beautiful nose, for example, is one that is neither very long nor very short, neither very straight nor very crooked, but a sort of middle among all those extremes, and less different from any one of them than all of them are from one another. It is the form which Nature seems to have aimed at in them all, which, however, she deviates from in a great variety of ways, and very seldom hits exactly; but to which all those deviations still bear a very strong resemblance. When a number of drawings are made after one pattern, though they may all miss it in some respects, yet they will all resemble it more than they resemble one another; the general character of the pattern will run through them all; the most singular and odd will be those which are most wide of it; and though very few will copy it exactly, yet the most accurate delineations will bear a greater resemblance to the most careless, than the careless ones will bear to one another. In the same manner, in each species of creatures, what is most beautiful bears the strongest characters of the general fabric of the species, and has the strongest resemblance to the greater part of the individuals with which it is classed. Monsters, on the contrary, or what is perfectly deformed, are always most singular and odd, and have the least resemblance to the generality of that species to which they belong. And thus the beauty of each species, though in one sense the rarest of all things, because few individuals hit this middle form exactly, yet in another is the most common, because all the deviations from it resemble it more than they resemble one another. The most customary form therefore is, in each species of things, according to him, the most beautiful. And hence it is that a certain practice and experience in contemplating each species of objects is requisite, before we can judge of its beauty, or know wherein the middle and most usual form consists. The nicest judgment concerning the beauty of the human species will not help us to judge of that of flowers or horses, or any other species of things.

Source Excerpted from Smith, A. (1966). *The theory of moral sentiments.* New York: Augustus M. Kelley. (Original work published 1759)

Biographical note Adam Smith (1723–1790) was an eighteenth-century Scottish moral philosopher. He became a professor of Logic at Glasgow, and eventually the Chair of the Moral Philosophy. He left the university in 1764 to tutor the Duke of Buccleuch. He is best known for his book, *Wealth of Nations* (1776), where he discussed a variety of issues pertaining to economics, such as education, commerce, labor, and politics.

* * *

The Economic Theory of Woman's Dress
Thorstein B. Veblen

... The line of progress during the initial stage of the evolution of apparel was from the simple concept of adornment of the person by supplementary accessions from without, to the complex concept of an adornment that should render the person pleasing, or of an enviable presence, and at the same time serve to indicate the possession of other virtues than that of a well-favored person only. In this latter direction lies what was to evolve into dress. By the time dress emerged from the primitive efforts of the savage to beautify himself with gaudy additions to his person, it was already an economic factor of some importance. The change from a purely aesthetic character (ornament) to a mixture of the aesthetic and economic took place before the progress had been achieved from pigments and trinkets to what is commonly understood by apparel. Ornament is not properly an economic category, although the trinkets which serve the purpose of ornament may also do duty as an economic factor, and in so far be assimilated to dress. What constitutes dress an economic fact, properly falling within the scope of economic theory, is its function as an index of the wealth of its wearer – or, to be more precise, of its owner, for the wearer and owner are not necessarily the same person. It will hold with respect to more than one half the values currently recognized as "dress," especially that portion with which this paper is immediately concerned – woman's dress that the wearer and the owner are different persons. But while they need not be united in the same person, they must be organic members of the same economic unit; and the dress is the index of the wealth of the economic unit which the wearer represents.

Under the patriarchal organization of society, where the social unit was the man (with his dependents), the dress of the women was an exponent of the wealth of the man whose chattels they were. In modern society, where the unit is the household, the woman's dress sets forth the wealth of the household to which she belongs. Still, even to-day, in spite of the nominal and somewhat celebrated demise of the patriarchal idea, there is that about the dress of women which suggests that the wearer is something in the nature of a chattel; indeed, the theory of woman's dress quite plainly involves the implication that the woman is a chattel. In this respect the dress of women differs from that of men. With this exception, which is not of first-rate importance, the essential principles of woman's dress are not different from those which govern the dress of men; but even apart from this added characteristic the element of dress is to be seen in a more unhampered development in the apparel of women. A discussion of the theory of dress in general will gain in brevity and conciseness by keeping in view the concrete facts of the highest manifestation of the principles with which it has to deal, and this highest manifestation of dress is unquestionably seen in the apparel of the women of the most advanced modern communities.

. . . Woman, primarily, originally because she was herself a pecuniary possession, has become in a peculiar way the exponent of the pecuniary strength of her social group; and with the progress of specialization of functions in the social organism this duty tends to devolve more and more entirely upon the woman. The best, most advanced, most highly developed

Figure 8.1 ". . . the dress is the index of the wealth of the economic unit which the wearer represents . . ." These fashionable and elaborate gowns of 1890 are excellent examples of Veblen's thesis that dress can be used as the index of a household's wealth. Of Parisian design, they are made of silk with copious trimmings and complex underpinnings in the shelf-bustle style. Fashion Plate – *Les Modes Parisiennes*. From *Peterson's Magazine*, May, 1890, Philadelphia: C.J. Peterson.

societies of our time have reached the point in their evolution where it has (ideally) become the great, peculiar, and almost the sole function of woman in the social system to put in evidence her economic unit's ability to pay. That is to say, woman's place (according to the ideal scheme of our social system) has come to be that of a means of conspicuously unproductive expenditure.

The admissible evidence of the woman's expensiveness has considerable range in respect of form and method, but in substance it is always the same. It may take the form of manners, breeding, and accomplishments that are, *prima facie*, impossible to acquire or maintain without such leisure as bespeaks a considerable and relatively long-continued possession of wealth. It may also express itself in a peculiar manner of life, on the same grounds and with much the same purpose. But the method in vogue always and everywhere, alone or in conjunction with other methods, is that of dress. "Dress," therefore, from the economic point of view, comes pretty near being synonymous with "display of wasteful expenditure." . . .

. . . It is not that the wearers or the buyers of these wasteful goods desire the waste. They desire to make manifest their ability to pay. What is sought is not the *de facto* waste, but the appearance of waste. Hence there is a constant effort on the part of the consumers of these goods to obtain them at as good a bargain as may be; and hence also a constant effort on the part of the producers of these goods to lower the cost of their production, and consequently to lower the price. But as fast as the price of the goods declines to such a figure that their consumption is no longer *prima facie* evidence of a considerable ability to pay, the particular goods in question fall out of favor, and consumption is diverted to something which more adequately manifests the wearer's ability to afford wasteful consumption . . .

Source Excerpted from Veblen, T.B. (1894). The economic theory of women's dress. *Popular Science Monthly, 46,* 198–205.

* * *

Dress as an Expression of the Pecuniary Culture
Thorstein B. Veblen

It will be in place, by way of illustration, to show in some detail how the economic principles so far set forth apply to everyday facts in some one direction of the life process. For this purpose no line of consumption affords a more apt illustration than expenditure on dress. It is especially the rule of the conspicuous waste of goods that finds expression in dress, although the other, related principles of pecuniary repute are also exemplified in the same contrivances. Other methods of putting one's pecuniary standing in evidence serve their end effectually, and other methods are in vogue always and everywhere; but expenditure on dress has this advantage over most other methods, that our apparel is always in evidence and affords an indication of our pecuniary standing to all observers at the first glance. It is also true that admitted expenditure for display is more obviously present, and is, perhaps, more universally practised in the matter of dress than in any other line of consumption. No one finds difficulty in assenting to the commonplace that the greater part of the expenditure incurred by all classes for apparel is incurred for the sake of a respectable appearance rather than for the protection of the person. And probably at no other point is the sense of shabbiness so keenly felt as it is if we fall short of the standard set by social usage in this matter of dress. It is true of dress in even a higher degree than of most other items of consumption, that people will undergo a very considerable degree of privation in the comforts or the necessaries of life in order to afford what is considered a decent amount of wasteful consumption; so that it is by no means an uncommon occurrence, in an inclement climate, for people to go ill clad in order to appear well dressed. And the commercial value of the goods used for clothing in any modern community is made up to a much larger extent of the fashionableness, the reputability of the goods than of the mechanical service which they render in clothing the person of the wearer. The need of dress is eminently a "higher" or spiritual need.

This spiritual need of dress is not wholly, nor even chiefly, a naïve propensity for display of expenditure. The law of conspicuous waste guides consumption in apparel, as in other things, chiefly at the second remove, by shaping the canons of taste and decency. In the common run of cases the conscious motive of the wearer or purchaser of conspicuously wasteful apparel is the need of conforming to established usage, and of living up to the accredited standard of taste and reputability. It is not only that one must be guided by the code of proprieties in dress in order to avoid the mortification that comes of unfavorable notice and comment, though that motive in itself counts for a great deal; but besides that, the requirement of expensiveness is so ingrained into our habits of thought in matters of dress that any other than expensive apparel is instinctively odious to us. Without reflection or analysis, we feet that what is inexpensive is unworthy. "A cheap coat makes a cheap man." " Cheap and nasty" is recognized to hold true in dress with even less mitigation than in other lines of consumption. On the ground both of taste and of service-ability, an inexpensive article of apparel is held to be inferior, under the maxim "cheap and nasty." We find things beautiful, as well as serviceable, somewhat in proportion as they are costly. With few and inconsequential exceptions, we all find a costly hand-wrought article of apparel much preferable, in point of beauty and of serviceability, to a less expensive imitation of it, however cleverly the spurious article may imitate the costly original; and what offends our sensibilities in the spurious article is not that it falls short in form or color, or, indeed, in visual effect in any way. The offensive object, may be so close an imitation as to defy any but the closest scrutiny; and yet so soon as the counterfeit is detected, its aesthetic value, and its commercial value as well, declines precipitately. Not only that, but it may be asserted with but small risk of contradiction that the aesthetic value of a detected counterfeit in dress declines somewhat in the same proportion as the counterfeit is cheaper than its original. It loses caste aesthetically because it falls to a lower pecuniary grade.

But the function of dress as an evidence of ability to pay does not end with simply showing that the wearer consumes valuable goods in excess of what is required for physical comfort. Simple conspicuous waste of goods is effective and gratifying as far as it goes; it is good *prima facie* evidence of pecuniary success, and consequently *prima facie* evidence of social worth. But dress has subtler and more far-reaching possibilities than this crude, first-hand evidence of wasteful consumption only. If, in addition to showing that the wearer can afford to consume freely and uneconomically, it can also be shown in the same stroke that he or she is not under the necessity of earning a livelihood, the evidence of social worth is enhanced in a very considerable degree. Our dress, therefore, in order to serve its purpose effectually, should not only be expensive, but it should also make plain to all observers that the wearer is not engaged in any kind of productive labor. In the evolutionary process by which our system of dress has been elaborated into its present admirably perfect adaptation to its purpose, this subsidiary line of evidence has received due attention. A detailed examination of what passes in popular apprehension for elegant apparel will show that it is contrived at every point to convey the impression that the wearer does not habitually put forth any useful effort. It goes without saying that no apparel can be considered elegant, or even decent, if it shows the effect of manual labor on the part of the wearer, in the way of soil or wear. The pleasing effect of neat and spotless garments is chiefly, if not altogether, due to their carrying the suggestion of leisure – exemption from personal contact with industrial processes of any kind. Much of the charm that invests the patent-leather shoe, the stainless linen, the lustrous cylindrical hat, and the walking-stick, which so greatly enhance the native dignity of a gentleman, comes of their pointedly suggesting that the wearer cannot when so attired bear a hand in any employment that is directly and immediately of any human use. Elegant dress serves its purpose of elegance not only in that it is expensive, but also because it is the insignia of leisure. It not only shows that the wearer is able to consume a relatively large value, but it argues at the same time that he consumes without producing.

The dress of women goes even farther than that of men in the way of demonstrating the wearer's abstinence from productive employment. It needs no argument to enforce the generalization that the more elegant styles of feminine bonnets go even farther towards making work impossible than does the man's high hat. The woman's shoe adds the so-called French heel to the evidence of enforced leisure afforded by its polish; because this high heel obviously makes any, even the simplest and most necessary manual work extremely difficult. The like is true even in a higher degree of the skirt and the rest of the drapery which characterizes woman's dress. The substantial reason for our tenacious attachment to the skirt is just this: it is expensive and it hampers the wearer at every turn and incapacitates her for all useful exertion. The like is true of the feminine custom of wearing the hair excessively long.

But the woman's apparel not only goes beyond that of the modern man in the degree in which it argues exemption from labor; it also adds a peculiar and highly characteristic feature which differs in kind from anything habitually practised by the men. This feature is the class of contrivances of which the corset is the typical example. The corset is, in economic theory, substantially a mutilation, undergone for the purpose of lowering the subject's vitality and rendering her permanently and obviously unfit for work. It is true, the corset impairs the personal attractions of the wearer, but the loss suffered on that score is offset by the gain in reputability which comes of her visibly increased expensiveness and infirmity. It may broadly be set down that the womanliness of woman's apparel resolves itself, in point of substantial fact, into the more effective hindrance to useful exertion offered by the garments peculiar to women. This difference between masculine and feminine apparel is here simply pointed out as a characteristic feature. The ground of its occurrence will be discussed presently.

So far, then, we have, as the great and dominant norm of dress, the broad principle of conspicuous waste. Subsidiary to this principle, and as a corollary under it, we get as a second norm the principle of conspicuous leisure. In dress construction this norm works out in the shape of divers contrivances going to show that the wearer does not and, as far as it may conveniently be shown, cannot engage in productive labor. Beyond these two principles there is a third of scarcely less constraining force, which will occur to any one who reflects at all on the subject. Dress must not only be conspicuously expensive and inconvenient; it must at the same time be up to date. No explanation at all satisfactory has hitherto been offered of the phenomenon of changing fashions. The imperative requirement of dressing in the latest accredited manner, as well as the fact that this accredited fashion constantly changes from season to season, is sufficiently familiar to every one, but the theory of this flux and change has not been worked out. We may of course say, with perfect consistency and truthfulness, that this principle of novelty is another corollary under the law of conspicuous waste. Obviously, if each garment is permitted to serve for but a brief term, and if none of last season's apparel is carried over and made further use of during the present season, the wasteful expenditure on dress is greatly increased. This is good as far as it goes, but it is negative only. Pretty much all that this consideration warrants us in saying is that the norm of conspicuous waste exercises a controlling surveillance in all matters of dress, so that any change in the fashions must conform to the requirement of wastefulness; it leaves unanswered the question as to the motive for making and accepting a change in the prevailing styles, and it also fails to explain why conformity to a given style at a given time is so imperatively necessary as we know it to be . . .

Source Excerpted from Veblen, T.B. (1899). *The theory of the leisure class.* New York: Macmillan.

Biographical note Thorstein Bunde Veblen (1857–1929) was an economist and social scientist. He received his Ph.D. from Yale in 1884, and taught at the University of Chicago, Stanford University, and The New School for Social Research. His theory of the leisure class reflects his fundamental views. Veblen believed that economics should be studied as an aspect of culture.

* * *

A Psychological Analysis of Fashion Motivation
Estelle de Young Barr

Overview of the General Problem

The psychology of choice is one of the most fundamental problems in applied social psychology. It is essentially the study of motivation, of attitudes and desires functioning as "coercive" and directive energies leading to acceptance-rejection responses.

It is the purpose of this investigation to study the practical problems of choice in the selection of women's clothes. For the sake of concreteness and comparability of data only the selection of the "daytime frock," a garment of general utility, is considered. This study is concerned with the complex of numerous varied factors in such selection, their relative potencies, their interrelationships and their conflicting and congruent effects on the resultant activity of choice.

. . . The choice of a dress is a major social activity. A study of this selective activity involves not only a consideration of the cultural pattern but of the individual as an element in the pattern. It involves also a consideration of the individual's awareness of the self as an entity, a Gestalt, within the total configuration.

The problem is concerned with such questions as: To what extent does the awareness of self involve self-analysis? How cognizant is the individual of the qualities and characteristics of the physical I and the I that is called personality? If self-analysis leads to awareness of the qualities that contribute to the total Gestalt, the prevalent mode determines the standard of beauty by which these qualities are judged acceptable or unacceptable. Clothes attitudes may be analyzed down to awareness of self, self-analysis, recognition of defects and the creation of an "ideal" self. Clothes are not only part of the self, but they are the means for expressing those traits which seem desirable. They are at once the instrument of self-expression and of conformity to an ideal. If a woman chooses clothes to present a certain picture of herself, the choice depends not only on a knowledge of self, but also on the perception of certain basic elements of design of the garment. Thus the desire for conformity, desire for self-expression and aesthetic preferences and judgements exert their influences on the selection of the dress, which is both an end and a means . . .

Fashion is sometimes compared to or contrasted with "custom" which, of course, has greater stability as well as wider scope. In general, fashion is defined as the "mode" in choices within a group; mode in a statistical sense. But, besides its connotations of conformity, popularity, prevalence and majority opinion, it is also recognized as being characterized by change often described as "cyclic," but not necessarily associated with progress. The modal elements might be considered centripetal and the cyclic elements centrifugal in their influences.

Suggestibility, imitativeness, desire to conform, desire for companionship and fear of social disapproval are some of the individual tendencies most often mentioned to account for this group modality in choices. Desire for the new, progress, desire for economic and social prestige and desire for leadership and self-assertion are some of the urges usually associated with change in fashion. Commercial interests and fashion experts are included among the factors which make for style change and style adoption.

Relative Importance of Group Attitudes

Of the fundamental attitudes involved in the psychology of choice of dress, the following are found to be among the more significant:

1. Desire to conform is the most diffuse of the desires measured; is more effective as a motive in determining the time of buying than desire for economy, and varies in intensity with the technical or professional interest of the group.
2. Desire for comfort with respect to temperature and tactual sensations is very important.
3. Modesty, though a significant factor, is not a very important motive for resisting a new fashion (brassiere bathing suit). Desire for comfort

(freedom of movement), aesthetic standards, awareness of physical style defects, desire for conformity, are other factors creating resistance.

4. Desire for economy is very widespread as an attitude but as a motive in determining time of buying is less effective than the desire to conform.

5. The aesthetic impulse is very important in the choice of a dress and functions in conjunction with the desire to be beautiful and the desire for conformity.

Of the constellation of fundamental attitudes related to the desire for self-expression:

1. Awareness of the physical self is very important in the choice of clothes.
2. Desire to be beautiful is important and operates in conjunction with the desire to conform.
3. The expression of different personality traits through the choice of a dress is of variable importance:

Desire to express "personality" is of more than moderate importance.
Desire to appear distinctive is of moderate importance.
Desire to appear dignified or youthful is of barely moderate importance.
Desire to appear competent is of less than moderate importance.
Desire to appear prosperous is of very little importance.

The most important factor determining the place of purchase is direct experience or experimental investigation rather than advertisements or recommendation.

Sources of style knowledge are of variable importance to the different groups. Reading sources are on the average, among the more important; social sources are among the less important.

Fashion knowledge is approximately commensurate with reading habits and technical interest in fashion.

Conclusions

. . . The following conclusions are drawn from the results of this investigation:

The really fundamental attitudes in the choice of clothes – those associated with the desire to conform, desire for comfort, desire for economy, the artistic impulse, and with self expression through sex and femininity – occur so positively and so widely diffused as to seem to be "universal." They cut across differences in educational backgrounds, in economic status, in reading habits, in amount of technical fashion knowledge and in professional interest in fashion.

Most differences in attitudes involve differences in the intensity of the desire to be in fashion and in the more specific and practical expression of the fundamental attitudes.

Awareness of the physical Gestalt and a definite desire to attain to ideals of slenderness and tallness, particularly by those who deviate most from the standards of beauty set by fashion, are keen. Attitudes are naturally very closely interwoven and interact functionally on each other. The choice of particular design elements in a dress may at once express the individual's ideas of what is beautiful, the desire to conform to the prevailing mode and the desire to be beautiful through creating the illusion of beauty of form and through enhancing personal coloring with clothes colors.

The desire to be beautiful is evidenced by the choice of design elements of dress effective in creating the illusion of beauty of form and by the choice of colors to enhance the tones of the physical self.

The desire to express personality is very widely diffused, although such individual personality characteristics as distinctiveness, youthfulness and dignity seem to be of barely moderate importance as objectives in the choice of a dress. Expression of the economic or social traits – the desire to appear competent or affluent – seems to be definitely negative as motivating factors.

The attitudes involved in the expression of the self do not differ significantly as between different groups.

An index of the importance which the choice of a dress assumes in the mind of the consumer is the amount of time and effort expended in window-shopping and shopping around, which more often than advertisements or recommendation directly determine the place where to buy.

Advertising seems to be more potent as a source of fashion ideas than as a direct stimulus to buying. Discrepancies in advertising practice and consumer attitudes may account in part, though not entirely, for this loss in effectiveness.

Source Excerpted from Barr, E. (1934). A psychological analysis of fashion motivation. *Archives of Psychology*, 26, 1–100.

Biographical note Estelle de Young Barr (1893–1979) was a psychologist who received her academic training at Barnard College, University of Pittsburgh, New School for Social Workers in New York City, and Columbia University, where she received her doctorate. She worked in several clinical settings as a psychologist.

Chronological Annotated Bibliography (1575–1940)

Those entries marked with an asterisk (*) are excerpted readings included in the text. All of the readings have been annotated with the exception of those that are presented in their entirety.

*1575. de Montaigne, M. (1927). *The essays of Montaigne.* (Vol. 1). London: Oxford University Press. (Original work published 1575)

The reading is presented in its entirety.

*1759. Smith, A. (1966). *The theory of moral sentiments.* New York: Augustus M. Kelley. (Original work published 1759)

In Smith's theory, the principles of custom and fashion both control human judgments of beauty. As social behaviors, fashion and custom are important to Smith's theory in which morality is a matter of social interaction. Custom establishes the general rules, and fashion gives grace and character to social conduct and good taste. As discussed in the excerpt, ideas of fashion as continuous rapid change apply to such objects of taste as dress, furniture, music, poetry, and architecture.

*1818. Hazlitt, W. (1818). On fashion. *The Edinburgh Magazine.*

Hazlitt in this article notes the power of fashion. As fashion spreads to the masses it lessens its influence. Fashion, according to Hazlitt begins and ends in two things: "singularity and vulgarity . . . first setting up the style and then disowning it." Hazlet remarks on the communicative power of dress through his comment that "dress is the great secret of address" (1818, p. 55).

1833. Carlyle, T. (1908). *Sartor resartus.* New York: Charles Scribner's Sons. (Original work published 1833)

In this book Carlyle poses as an editor preparing a collection of material for publication. The philosophy of clothes operates as an elaborate metaphor allowing Carlyle to develop his philosophy about man's place in the universe.

*1856. Fry, M.E. (1856). Let us have a national costume. *The Ladies Repository,* 16, 735–738.

Fry is calling for dress reform. She is advocating a national costume, a style that reflects U.S. values and identity rather than importing styles from other countries.

*1872. Darwin, G.H. (1872). Development in dress. *Macmillan's Magazine, 26,* 410–416.

Darwin is applying evolutionary theory to explain changes in styles of clothing. He contends that forms of clothing are evolving to better styles and clothing that ceases to have a function is handed down in atrophied conditions.

1877. Blanc, C. (1877). *Art in ornament and dress.* New York: Scriber, Wilfred-Armstrong.

The principles of repetition, alternation, progression, symmetry, and confusion found in nature have been and will continue to serve as the basis for dressing the body.

*1881. Flower, W.H. (1881). *Fashion in deformity.* London: Macmillan.

Flower defines the word deformity and gives his view on the evolution and adoption of clothing styles. The motive behind the prevailing fashions is the need not to appear singular. He notes that the most civilized peoples practice some of the most absurd fashions. He offers suggestions for improvements on dress styles.

*1885. Ballin, A.S. (1885). *The science of dress in theory and practice.* London: Sampson, Low, Marston, Searle, and Rivington.

Ballin discusses dress and dress reform in relation to health. Her book is a treatise on the unhealthy effects of fabrics, colors and dyes, the weight of garments, and restrictive undergarments on the bodies of women and children. Ballin proposes her system as a science of dress based on a classic Greek ideal of health and beauty. Her ultimate goal is to make clothing both healthy and fashionable so that her system will find success.

*1887. Lotze, R.H. (1887). *Microcosmos: An essay concerning man and his relation to the world.* Edinburgh: T.T. Clark.

Lotze uses human satisfaction in dress and clothing as a means to present his philosophical ideas and work on the theory of knowledge and reality. According to Lotze, human beings perceive and learn about the world and the universe on a physical level, through their bodies and clothing. Clothing gives sensations and feelings of existence, and is used to convey impressions and personality and both embody and modify the world outside the human body.

1892. Russell, F.E. (1892). A brief survey of American dress reform movement of the past with views of representative women. *The Arena, 6*(33), 325–339.

Russell reflects on several articles that address issues relating to women's dress including dress reform from the perspective both of women's health and of improving the condition of women.

1893. Foley, C.A. (1893). Fashion. *Economic Journal, 3,* 458–474.

Foley notes in her discussion of fashion that fashion results from conformity in behavior. She contends that when customs are stable change in dress is slower.

*1894. Veblen, T.B. (1894). The economic theory of women's dress. *Popular Science Monthly, 46,* 198–205.

Veblen in this reading presents his view of the purpose of dress. According to Veblen people dress they way they do for comfort (which in his view is an afterthought) and for economic reasons. Veblen focuses his presentation on the economic reasons. The excerpt provides his main arguments.

*1895. Bloomer, A. (1975). In Dexter C. Bloomer, *The life and writings of Amelia Bloomer*. New York: Shocken Books. (Original work published 1895)

This excerpt is drawn from the book written after her death by Amelia Bloomer's husband. In addition to biographical information and chapters about her travels and relationships with women's suffrage contemporaries, Dexter Bloomer included generous excerpts from Bloomer's own writings and commentaries about Bloomer and her work written by her contemporaries.

*1896. Spencer, H. (1924). *The principles of sociology*. New York and London: Appleton. (Original work published 1896)

Spencer views clothing as a method of communication. Clothing is also intrinsically imitative and serves to obliterate marks of class distinction.

*1898. Hall, G.S. (1898). Some aspects of the early sense of self. *American Journal of Psychology, 9,* 351–395.

Hall writes about the functions of clothing: protection, ornamentation, and Lotzean self-feeling. He examines clothing in relationship to self and self-development. The discussion outlines what Hall believes to be the evolution of the development of self-consciousness. The excerpt is taken from a larger discussion of what Hall believes is the progression that children follow in developing an awareness of what is a part of their body and what aspects of their bodies they control and what is outside of bodily self. The excerpt focuses on the role that dress plays in the development of self.

1899. Thomas, W.I. (1899). The psychology of modesty and clothing. *American Journal of Sociology, 5*, 246–262.

Thomas is examining the relationships between modesty and clothing. The focus of his thesis in this article is that modesty comes about as a result of the habit of wearing clothing.

*1899. Veblen, T.B. (1899). *The theory of the leisure class.* New York: Macmillan Company.

Veblen provides definitions to distinguish between the terms clothing and dress. He contends that dress is an indicator of social status and women's dress in particular, reflects not her own social status but those of her family namely, her husband's or father's. His view is that dress reflects conspicuous waste.

*1904. Simmel, G. (1904). Fashion. *International Quarterly, 10*, 130–155.

Simmel discusses one of the theories of fashion diffusion – the trickle-down theory. He views fashion as a process of innovation followed by emulation. The process reflects an attempt at social equalization but because change never ends, fashion segregates. Simmel offers explanations for why ugly items become fashions, why some individuals do not participate in fashion, and under what conditions fashion actually exists. The excerpt focuses on his explanation for fashion change.

*1906. Flaccus, L.W. (1906). Remarks on the psychology of clothes. *The Pedagogical Seminary, 13*, 61–83.

Flaccus is using the data gathered in research by G. Stanley Hall to make some observations on the psychology of clothing. The data were gathered from girls enrolled in a normal school in the state of New York. He divided the participants responses into three groups: Minor and incidental matters, changes of self-feeling, and effects of the self as a social reflex phenomenon. Presented in the excerpt are his opening remarks and concluding statements as well as recommendations for needed research in the area.

1907. Webb, W.M. (1907). *The heritage of dress.* London: E.G. Richards.

Webb describes his book as "a popular contribution to the natural history of man" (1907, p. ix). The writing focuses on the application of the principles of evolution to clothing. His presentation focuses on several examples of clothing. He also addresses body modifications and dress reform.

*1908. Thomas, W.I. (1908). The psychology of women's dress. *The American Magazine, 67*, 66–72.

Thomas in this reading is addressing motives for dress as well as outlining the role of dress in society. He explains for the reader why men's dress has become somber while women's dress has increased in ornamentation. His main thesis is presented in the excerpt.

*1912. Crawley, A.E. (1912). Dress. *Encyclopedia of religion and ethics* (Vol. 5, pp. 40–72). New York: Charles Scribner's Sons.

Crawley defines dress as a second skin, as both an extension of the passive area of a person and of personality. He notes that the main problem in studying the origins of and motives for wearing clothes is not the invention of dress but the process of invention. Although analyzed as an evolutionary question, Crawley says that dress seems to have come into use all of a piece. He looks at how dress functions in numerous cultural settings, how dress changes as social roles change, and how dress reflects those changes.

1913. Clerget, P. (1913). The economic and social role of fashion. *Smithsonian Institution Report*, 755–765.

Clerget in his treatment of the economic and social role of fashion notes that fashion is a social custom that is transmitted by imitation or by tradition. He also addresses the cyclic nature of fashion and the issue of conspicuous consumption.

1915. Freud, S. (1943). Symbolism in dreams [from lectures in Vienna 1915–1917]. In S. Freud and J. Riviere (trans), *General introduction to psychoanalysis* (pp. 133–145). Garden City and New York: Garden City Publishing Co. (Original work published 1920)

Freud's work in this volume is drawn from lectures prepared for presentations to the general public, not to psychology students or scientific colleagues. He describes clothing symbolism as it is used in dream interpretation for mentally disturbed patients. In Freud's work, the human body is symbolized as a house, and clothes or uniforms symbolize nakedness. Various clothing symbols, such as hats and cloaks, represent sexual symbols.

*1916. Bliss, S.H. (1916). The significance of clothes. *American Journal of Psychology*, 27, 217–226.

In this discussion Bliss attempts to answer the question of why humans wear clothes. Why did humans feel a need to add to what nature provided? She refutes several of the contemporary theories and presents her own views. She contends that humans got dressed due to feelings of incompleteness. Humans are dissatisfied with our bodies as they are and clothing in its origin is at attempt to remedy the situation. Her view is evolutionary in nature. We present in this excerpt her main arguments.

*1918. Dearborn, G.V.N. (1918). The psychology of clothing. *The Psychological Monographs*, 26, 1–72.

Dearborn reflects on both the physiological and the applied psychological aspects of dress. He is attempting to locate scientific laws that will be applicable to dressing the body. He examines the relationship between clothing and the skin. He views clothing as intervening between the body and the larger environment as well as impacting humans spiritually. In the reading he addresses the relationships of clothing to the skin, reasons for the development of clothes, and the psychology of clothing including presenting some early ideas on the importance of dress for social advancement. The excerpt presents his ideas on the physiologic aspects of clothing.

1919. Kroeber, A.L. (1919). On the principle of order in civilization as exemplified by changes of fashion. *The American Anthropologist, 21,* 235–263.

Kroeber, in order to better understand civilization, in this article is looking for the principles that guide fashion. His approach is to measure illustrations of women's dress. He used fashion plates that were idealized depictions of women's clothing styles.

1920. Parsons, F.A. (1920). *The psychology of dress.* Garden City and New York: Doubleday, Page, and Company.

The book presents a history of France, England, Italy, and the United States from the twelfth century to the present, illustrated through the lives of the rulers, their dress, and housing. Parsons outlines his views on clothing, including the notion that clothing was the first receptacle of art, the use of clothing to attract attention, and communication of social status. He contends that the personal expression through clothing by some is only possible through the oppression of others. He also notes that although sumptuary laws are written, people reject them, and it is difficult, if not impossible, to regulate human display.

1922. Malinowski, B. (1961). *Argonauts of the western Pacific.* London. (Original work published in 1922)

In this reading Malinowski outlines what to consider in a functional analysis of a culture. He notes that the physical world of the individual must be taken into account along with the body of tools and commodities produced. He presents what he views as the biological and derived needs of humans and how humans meet these needs. He notes that humans develop dress in response to a need for bodily comforts.

*1922. Radcliffe-Brown, Sir A.R. (1922). *The Andaman Islanders.* Cambridge: Cambridge University Press.

Radcliffe-Brown's work presented in the book is based on his fieldwork with the Andaman Islanders near the Bay of Bengal, India. He is exploring, in general, the meaning of personal ornament. According to Radcliffe-Brown, our sense of self attaches to our clothing and ornament, and can therefore transfer sensations to us symbolically. Amulets used for protection from evil are one example of this. He proposes two motives for the use of personal ornament – desires for protection and for display.

1924. Bogardus, E.S. (1924). Social psychology of fads. *Journal of Applied Sociology, 8,* 239–243.

Bogardus provides an analysis of fads that he conducted over a 10-year period. He notes that fads are located in superficial aspects of life and that the life of a fad is generally about 2 to 3 months but definitely not lasting more than one year. Fads exist in several aspects of life.

1924. Heard, G. (1924). *Narcissus: An anatomy of clothes*. London: Kegan Paul Trench Trubner.

Heard uses a theory labeled projected evolution. The theory states that human kind has evolved to a point where humans do not change but through their intelligence they continue the evolutionary procession in architecture and dress.

*1926. Morton, G.M. (1926). Psychology of dress. *Journal of Home Economics, 18*, 484–486.

Morton reflects on the psychological value of clothing. The reading is presented in its entirety.

1927. Sanborn, H.C. (1927). The function of clothing and of bodily adornment. *The American Journal of Psychology, 38*(1), 1–20.

Sanborn in this reading shares his views on origins of clothing. He discusses several perspectives including dress as a response to a need to attract sexual attention, as a need for modesty, as protection from the physical environment, and as a need for aesthetic expression.

*1928. Dunlap, K. (1928). The development and function of clothing. *Journal of General Psychology, 1*, 64–78.

Dunlap in this reading points out what are the four important theories concerning the origin of clothing. He discusses each with a view to determining their relevance to contemporary behavior. He then proceeds to a discussion of why clothing persists if not for reasons of health, modesty, and the like. The excerpt presents the main components of Dunlap's view on the function of clothing for both men and women.

1928. Nystrom, P. (1928). *Economics of fashion*. New York: Ronald Press.

Nystrom presents definitions of key terms including style and fashion. He discusses factors that influence fashion change and traces the origins and developments of "modern" fashion in apparel, home furnishings, and industrial innovation.

1929. Flügel, J.C. (1929). Clothes symbolism and clothes ambivalence. *International Journal of Psycho-Analysis, 10*, 205–217.

Flügel is influenced by the work of Sigmund Freud. He examines the conscious and unconscious use of clothing as well as symbolic aspects of various items of clothing. Flügel presents three classes of symbols: phallic, vaginal, and uterine. His unconscious motives for clothing include modesty, protection, and display.

1929. Hiler, H. (1929). *From nudity to raiment*. London: W. and G. Foyle.

Hiler's book provides an introduction to the history of dress based on almost 1,000 collected references to clothing and adornment in the literature of numerous disciplines. His stated purpose was to place costume in its proper position among the arts. He emphasizes the long prehistory of dress prior to the Egyptian civilization. Hiler proposed the study of costume as an indication of the stages of civilization.

*1929. Hurlock, E.B. (1929). Motivation in fashion. *Archives of Psychology, 17*(3), 5–71.

Hurlock does an investigation of the motives involved in clothing selection. She collects data over a period of several years and tests other writers' hypotheses about why people wear what they wear. Hurlock presents an overview of contemporary views on fashion motivations, the development of her questionnaire, and the results of her analysis.

1929. Hurlock, E.B. (1929). *The psychology of dress*. New York: Ronald Press.

Hurlock's book presents an expanded background and historical analysis for her study on motivation. She defines the fashion impulse as a democratic social force, and postulates that war, commercial interests, cross-cultural contact, and technology all contribute to the speed of change. In general, fashion can't be predicted, but styles are recycled approximately every 100 years. Hurlock discusses fashion as a mirror of the period, and states that general trends of thought and feeling are best shown in dress.

1930. Flügel, J.C. (1930). On the mental attitude to present-day clothes. *British Journal of Medical Psychology, 2*(9), 97–149.

Flügel reports on research he conducted with men and women that examined physical and social aspects of clothing. In this work Flügel distinguishes different types of persons: prudish, protected, supported, skin and muscle eroticism, and self-satisfied.

1931. Dooley, W.H. (1931). *Clothing and style*. New York: D.C. Heath.

Dooley addresses a variety of topics including apparel production, care, history, aesthetics, and psychology. He offers a detailed view with the underlying intention that people be knowledgeable about clothing so they select clothing that is appropriate for them.

*1931. Benedict, R. (1931). Dress. *Encyclopedia of the social sciences* (Vol. 5, 235–237). New York: Macmillan.

Benedict is defining the concept of dress. This reading is presented in its entirety.

*1931. Sapir, E. (1931). Fashion. *Encyclopedia of the social sciences* (Vol. 6, 139–144). New York: Macmillan.

Sapir attempts to define the concept of fashion. He begins by differentiating the concept fashion from other related terms. He then proceeds to address what fashion is and how it functions in society. The excerpt focuses on his ideas about fashion change.

1931. Vincent, J.M. (1931). Sumptuary legislation. *Encyclopedia of the social sciences* (Vol. 14, 464–466). New York: Macmillan.

Vincent addresses sumptuary legislation explaining their purpose and indicating that these laws are difficult to enforce. He explains the difference between sumptuary laws and "modern" tariffs, suggesting that the motives behind each are different.

1932. Flügel, J.C. (1932). *The psychology of clothes.* London: Hogarth.

Flügel outlines for the reader his view of the purposes of clothing: decoration, modesty, and protection. Flügel also introduces two principle types of development in clothing: modish and fixed, suggesting that the first is faster in evolutionary change than the latter.

1932. Harnik, E.J. (1932). Pleasure in disguise: The need for decoration and the sense of beauty. *Psychoanalytic Quarterly, 1,* 216–264.

Harnik takes a case-study approach to determine the origins of what he labels sexual peculiarities. His argument focuses on the castration complex and its relationship to fetishism and transvestism. He offers explanations for several aspects of dressing the body including tattooing.

*1934. Barr, E. de Young. (1934). A psychological analysis of fashion motivation. *Archives of Psychology, 26,* 1–100.

The excerpt comes from Barr's Ph.D. dissertation in which she studied the practical problems of choice in the selection of women's clothes. Barr looked at fashion motivation from the consumer's point of view, measuring the importance of attitudes, the effectiveness of attitudes as motives in clothing choice, and the relationship between these two. Her goal was to develop a picture of fashion as a complex dynamic system.

1937. Elliot, H. (1937). *Fashions in art.* New York: Appleton-Century.

Elliot provides a broad overview of types of art focusing on fine art and architecture. Although dress is mentioned at times, it is not a focus of this work. However, his ideas can be applied to dress including his notion that in order to understand art one needs to be aware of the context and the prevalent ideas of the time.

*1937. Laver, J. (1937). *Taste and fashion: From the French revolution until today.* London: G.G. Harrap.

With 1789 as starting point, Laver provides a chronological background of fashion in the first half of his book, discussing influences and sociological trends for changes in fashions and tastes. In the last chapter he develops his theory on fashion change and its connection to changes in taste in interiors and architecture. According to Laver, clothes serve two purposes – self-assertion and self-protection. The clothing of each period in history reflects the *zeitgeist* of that period.

*1937. Young, A.B. (1937). *Recurring cycles of fashion.* New York: Harper and Brothers.

Young's book is a statistical study of trends in women's fashions. According to Young, changes in women's fashion follow fixed and predictable patterns. By tracing historical evidence in fashion plates and magazines, she proposes a series of three well-defined and recurring cycles in skirt silhouettes of 38 to 40 years each. Young proposes that the psychological benefits of fashion change are to satisfy such needs as social position and recognition, and women's competition for male sexual attraction.

1938. Harms, E. (1938). The psychology of clothes. *American Journal of Sociology, 44*, 239–250.

Harms discusses several motives for dressing the body. He discusses modesty, protection, and adornment as fundamental motives. His argument is that while these motives offer some explanation, the fundamental motivation is the environment. Although the purpose of clothing is determined by environmental conditions, its form is determined by human characteristics and mental traits.

1939. Hawes, E. (1939). *Fashion is spinach.* New York: Random House.

Hawes outlines the apparel industry in Paris from her position as a copyist. She notes the French governmental support of the industry and notes that the United States does not support the apparel industry in the same way. She reflects on the type and amount of difficulties she experiences with apparel manufacturers in the United States.

1938. Meiklejohn, H.E. (1938). Dresses – The impact of fashion on a business. In W.H. Hamilton (Ed.), *Price and price policies* (pp. 299-393). New York: McGraw-Hill.

Meiklejohn is addressing the question of value. How is the value of an object determined? As she answers her question she takes into account the impact of production on pricing and the impact of fashion. She calls for reform of the fashion industry.

*1939. Blumer, H. (1939). Fashion movements. In Robert Ezra Park (Ed.), *From collective behavior: An outline of the principles of sociology* (pp. 275-277). New York: Barnes and Noble.

The excerpt is taken from a larger chapter on social movements in Blumer's book. It is presented in its entirety.

*1939. Hiler, H. & Hiler, M. (1939). *Bibliography of costume*. New York: H.W. Wilson.

This extensive bibliography was drawn from a total of over 8400 works on dress, jewelry, and body modifications. It has an international scope and was written in a dictionary catalog format. In the preface and introduction, the authors discuss the origins of and motives for wearing clothing, and present the psychological, social, and ideological implications of dress.

1940. Crawford, M.D.C. (1940). *Philosophy in clothing*. New York: Brooklyn Museum.

This publication was written as a catalog for an exhibition of historic dress at the Brooklyn Museum. A major reason for the exhibition and Crawford's contribution was to establish a more fruitful relationship between the museum collection and the apparel industry. Crawford addresses the impact of the history of technology on the fashion industry and important American contributions such as the invention of the sewing machine.

1940. Richardson, J. & Kroeber, A.L. (1940). Three centuries of women's dress fashions. *Anthropological Records, 5*.

Richardson and Kroeber report on their quantitative research designed to explain style trends. They build upon the work of Kroeber (1919) and use data covering 332 years. They present their data in both tables and graphs.

Index

adolescence 111
  development 112
adornment 12, 19, 20, 94
aesthetics 18, 19, 40, 71, 130
  impulse 138
  sense, 103
  value, 134
amulets 31
anthropomorphic elements 106
appearance 110
  management, 69, 71
  personal 106
applied psychology of clothing 11, 12, 37, 38,
attitude 137, 138, 139

Ballin, A. 13, 14
Barr, E. De Young 95, 136
beauty 63, 64
  ideal 94
  standard 13
Benedict, R. 10
Bergson, H. 9, 19
Bliss, S.H. 8, 9, 12
Bloomer, A. 13
Blumer, H. 94
body
  action 39
  concealment 24
  modification 1, 13, 92
  painting 27, 28
  supplements 13, 21
  temperature 39
  thinness 64

Carlyle, T. 19
caste 36, 64
castration fear 35

circulation 57
class distinction 101, 105
claustraphobias 44
clothing
  as artificial skin 38
  as communication, 1, 10, 76
  as protection, 7, 8, 9, 10, 14, 19, 28, 29,
    42, 63, 65, 66, 47,
  origins, 31, 34, 93, 115
  philosophy 8, 18, 20
  protection hypothesis 24, 26
  second skin 23
  selection 93
collective behavior 91, 94, 136
collective unconscious 9
comfort 16, 38, 62, 138
conformity 136, 137 , 138
consciousness 42
  body 12, 86
  clothes 12, 47, 86
  somatic 43
conspicuous waste, 70, 81 135
consumer behavior 91
consumption
  conspicuous 133
  wasteful 133
corporeal existence 46
corseting 13
costume 11, 31
  bloomer 13, 14, 61
  national 70, 77
  sanitary 59
couturier 116
Crawley, A. 8, 9, 10, 12 35,
culture
  pecuniary 132
custom 8, 15, 137
  ceremonial 29

Darwin, C. 2, 3., 9, 18, 91
Darwin, G. 3, 91
Dearborn , G. 11, 12, 110
deformity 51, 56
democracy 70
descent of man 98
disease 57
dress
  as artificial covering 22
  as communication 95
  as concealment 65
  as decoration 9, 10, 18, 32, 103
  as diffusion 104
  as extending the body's capabilities 9,
    10
  as geographically differentiated, 32
  as habit 63
  as modification 94
  as self expression 137
  as temporally differentiated, 32
  as unhealthful 33
  body 7
  ceremonial 92
  court 92
  definition 1
  development 97, 98
  economic expression, 95
  marking 10
  morality 95
  origins and motives 3, 7, 8, 9, 10, 14, 18,
    21, 27
  rational 47
  reform 7, 13, 14, 65
  ritual 92
  sexual 26
  survivals, 99
Dunlap, K. 14 , 31
Durkheim, E. 39

ego 45
Eicher, J. B. 1
Ellis, H. 35
erogenous zones 93
evolution 18, 23, 92, 94, 97
  creative 9
  human 22
  of dress 25
  process 134

psychological 27
social 7, 14, 21, 23, 95
theory 91
exhibitionism 115
exhibitionist 31

fad 64
fashion
  as change, 69, 91, 92, 93, 109, 113, 114,
    116, 119 , 123
  concept, 93
  cyclic 137
  defining, 2
  as imitation, 69, 92, 137
  imitation, 51, 73
  innovation 73, 92
  industry, 70
  knowledge 138, 139
  leadership, 70
  meaning, 2
  motivation, 112, 136, 104, 105, 106,
    107, 109, 111, 139
  origin, 51
  selection 91,
  singularity 73
  system, 69,
  vulgarity, 73
first impressions, 110
Flaccus, L. 69, 71, 110
Flower, W. H. 13, 14
Freud, S. 35
Fry, M. 69, 70, 77

gestalt, 136, 139
golden lily 53

Hall, G. S. 10, 12, 71, 110
Haraucourt, E. 35
Hazlitt, W. 69, 74, 77
health 7, 13, 14, 17, 57, 62, 63, 64
heraldic display 32, 36
Hiler, H. 11
Hiler, M. 11
Hood, T. 39
human ecological approach 13
  expression, 107
Hurlock, E. 92
hygiene 51, 66

identity 14, 69, 70
immodest 39
impulse
  clothing 19
  decorative 23, 25
  erotic 32
instinct 41
  human 31
interpretative 3

Jenson, J. 35
Jung, C. 9

laws 23
  manmade 8, 11, 12, 16
  mechanical 23
  natural 8
Laver, J. 93
Lotze, R. H. 10, 12, 46, 47

magic, 31
Main, H. 82
mass production 33
material justification, 106
mental survivals 20
menton 2
Miller, E. S. 59
modesty 9, 11, 14, 24, 27, 30, 42, 63, 115
  false 24
  motive 138
Montaigne, M. 2, 8, 9, 11, 35
morality 63
Morton, G. 69, 71, 87
mutilation 20

national dress system 13
natural selection 91, 99
nudity 30

ornament 10, 14, 20, 19, 21, 23, 24, 27, 29,
    47, 70, 92 , 102 , 104, 130
  ornamentation 32, 42
  ornamentation hypothesis 24

pecuniary possession 95
personality, 69, 71, 88 , 139
  trait, 138
physiological cues 86

physiological factors 85
physiological psychology of clothing 11, 37,
    38, 39
pigmentation 22
pleasure 42
psychical life 85
polity 16
positivistic 3
power, 29, 69, 70
psychology of clothes, 71
prestige 36

Radcliffe–Brown, A. 10, 11
religion 16
Roach-Higgins, M.E. 1

sanitarian 13
Santayana 34
Sapir, E. 93
satisfaction-efficiency ratio 37
scarification 27, 28
science
  of clothes 37
  of dress 13
self 12, 48
  self-analysis, 137
  self-confidence, 111
  self-consciousness 12, 13, 27, 45 , 47
  self-display 32,
  self-decoration 30
  self-expression, 137, 138
  self-feeling 12, 23, 46, 47
  self, ideal 137
  self, libidinal 113
  self, physical 7, 47
  self, sense of 27
sentient soul 40
sexual
  attractiveness 27, 64, 70
  competition 14, 63, 65, 66
  decoration 22
  modesty 65, 66
  morality 65, 66
  protection 26
  selection 14, 63, 93
sexuality 93
shame 31
Simmel, G. 92 107

skin 39, 40, 43, 44, 56, 57, 58
  garment, 101
  dress, 101
Smith, A. 94
social
  currency 10
  darwinism 2, 3, 7, 8, 9
  class 92, 94
  display 9, 10
  life 29
  process 105
  system 131
  value 28
soul 44, 45
Spencer, H. 10 12 51, 92, 100, 104
Stanton, E. C. 61
status 14, 32, 92
  nakedness 101
Steele, V. 91
Stone, L. 62
style
  adoption, 137
  change 137
suffragist 13
suggestibilty 137
symbol
  fertility 30

tattooing 13
temperance 62

theory
  amuletic 35
  castration 36
  esthetic 35
  fashion change, 93
  mosaic 35
  possession 35
  protection, 28, 29, 30, 31, 32 , 115
  sexual attraction 10, 35
  taboo 35
  totemistic 35
  trickle-down 92
Thomas, W. I. 69, 70, 81,
trophies 32,35
turkish trousers 61

uniforms 92

value
  compensatory, 109
Veblen, T. 70, 81, 95, 131, 132, 136
  theory, 109

wardrobe consultant 71
wool 56, 57
woolen 58, 59
women's rights 13
  suffrage 62

Young, A. B. 94